SOUL ASTR

A Birth Chart Guide for Beginners to Discovering Your Zodiac Signs and Predictions for Relationships, Understand Behavioral Patterns for Self-Awareness and Spiritual Growth

Melissa Gomes

https://smartpa.ge/MelissaGomes

Table of Contents

TABLE OF CONTENTS	**3**
FREEBIES!	**9**
BONUS 1: FREE WORKBOOK - VALUE 12.95$	9
BONUS 2: FREE BOOK - VALUE 12.95$	10
BONUS 3: FREE AUDIOBOOK - VALUE 14.95$	10
JOIN MY REVIEW TEAM!	10
FOR ALL THE FREEBIES, VISIT THE FOLLOWING LINK:	11
I'M HERE BECAUSE OF YOU	**12**
CHAPTER 1: ASTROLOGY FUNDAMENTALS	**13**
CHAPTER 2: THE ELEMENTS AND MODALITIES	**20**
Cardinal Signs	*20*
Fixed Signs	*20*
Mutable Signs	*21*
ELEMENTS IN THE ZODIAC	21
Fire	*22*
Air	*22*
Earth	*23*
CHAPTER 3: THE SUN SIGNS	**24**
ARIES	24
TAURUS	25
GEMINI	26
CANCER	26
LEO	27
VIRGO	27
LIBRA	27
SCORPIO	28
SAGITTARIUS	29
CAPRICORN	29
AQUARIUS	29
PISCES	30
CHAPTER 4: ASCENDANT SIGNS AND DECANS	**31**
Aries	*32*
Taurus	*33*
Gemini	*34*

Cancer   *35*
Leo   *35*
Virgo   *36*
Libra   *37*
Scorpio   *37*
Sagittarius   *38*
Capricorn   *38*
Aquarius   *39*
Pisces   *39*
DECANS   40
March 21 to April 19: Aries   *41*
April 20 to May 20: Taurus   *41*
May 21 to June 20: Gemini   *42*
June 21 to July 22: Cancer   *42*
July 23 to August 22: Leo   *43*
August 23 to September 22: Virgo   *43*
September 23 to October 22: Libra   *44*
October 23 to November 21: Scorpio   *45*
November 22 to December 21: Sagittarius   *45*
December 22 to January 19: Capricorn   *46*
January 20 to February 18: Aquarius   *46*
February 19 to March 20: Pisces   *47*

CHAPTER 5: THE PLANETS AND OTHER CELESTIAL BODIES   **48**

SUN   48
MOON   49
MERCURY   50
VENUS   51
MARS   51
JUPITER   52
SATURN   53
URANUS   53
NEPTUNE   53
PLUTO   54
HEALING ASPECTS   55

CHAPTER 6: ASPECTS IN THE ZODIAC   **56**

CONJUNCTION   57
OPPOSITION   58
TRINE   59
SQUARE   60
SEMISQUARE   61

SESQUISQUARE   61
QUINTILE   61
SEMISEXTILE   62
SEXTILE   62
INCONJUNCT   62
HARMONIC CHARTS   63
HIGHLY ASPECTED PLANETS   63
  Essential Bodies   *64*

CHAPTER 7: THE ASTROLOGICAL HOUSES   65

FIRST HOUSE   66
SECOND HOUSE   66
THIRD HOUSE   67
FOURTH HOUSE   67
FIFTH HOUSE   67
SIXTH HOUSE   68
SEVENTH HOUSE   68
EIGHTH HOUSE   69
NINTH HOUSE   69
TENTH HOUSE   69
ELEVENTH HOUSE   70
TWELFTH HOUSE   70

CHAPTER 8: UNDERSTANDING YOUR BIRTH CHART   72

THE BIG THREE   74
  Sun   *74*
  The Moon   *75*
  Eclipses   *75*
THE FOUR PARTS ON YOUR BIRTH CHART   76
  Ascendant   *76*
  Descendant   *76*
  Midheaven   *76*
  Nadir   *77*
YOUR RULING PLANET   77
STELLIUM   78
  Mutually-Receptive Planets   *78*
CHIRON   AND NON-PLANETARY CELESTIAL OBJECTS   78
  Vesta   *79*
  Ceres   *80*
  Pallas Athena   *81*
  Juno   *81*

CHAPTER 9: YOUR BIRTH CHART INTERPRETATION   83

Nodes 83
    North Node 83
    South Node 85
    Lunar Nodes 87
Part of Fortune 88
Retrogrades 90
The Hemispheres 92
Eclipses 92
Transits 94

CHAPTER 10: YOUR ZODIAC SIGN'S QUALITIES   **96**

    Aries 96
    Taurus 97
    Gemini 98
    Cancer 99
    Leo 100
    Virgo 102
    Libra 103
    Scorpio 104
    Sagittarius 105
    Capricorn 106
    Aquarius 107
    Pisces 108
Compatibility in Love 109
    The Affectionate Aries 109
    The Loving Taurus 110
    The Romantic Gemini 111
    The Affectionate Cancer 111
    The Adoring Leo 112
    The Devoted Virgo 113
    The Caring Libra 114
    The Fond Scorpio 115
    The Supportive Sagittarius 116
    The Warmhearted Capricorn 116
    The Tender Aquarius 117
    The Big-Hearted Pisces 118
Conclusion 119

POSITIVE AFFIRMATIONS – PART 1   **120**

POSITIVE AFFIRMATIONS - PART 2   **124**

GUIDED MEDITATION   **127**

FREEBIES!   **130**

    BONUS 1: FREE WORKBOOK - VALUE 12.95$ 130
    BONUS 2: FREE BOOK - VALUE 12.95$ 131
    BONUS 3: FREE AUDIOBOOK - VALUE 14.95$ 131
    JOIN MY REVIEW TEAM!   131
    FOR ALL THE FREEBIES, VISIT THE FOLLOWING LINK: 132

I'M HERE BECAUSE OF YOU   **133**

MELISSA GOMES
LITTLEESPIRITUAL.COM

FREEBIES

AND

RELATED PRODUCTS

WORKBOOKS
AUDIOBOOKS
FREE BOOKS
REVIEW COPIES

HERE

HTTPS://SMARTPA.GE/MELISSAGOMES

Freebies!

I have a **special treat for you**! You can access exclusive bonuses I created specifically for my readers at the following link! The link will redirect you to a webpage containing all my books and bonuses for each book. Just select the book you have purchased and check the bonuses!

>> https://smartpa.ge/MelissaGomes<<

OR scan the QR Code with your phone's camera

Bonus 1: Free Workbook - Value 12.95$

This **workbook** will guide you with **specific questions** and give you all the space you need to write down the answers. Taking time for **self-reflection** is extremely valuable, especially when looking to develop new skills and **learn** new concepts. I highly suggest you *grab this complimentary workbook for yourself*, as it will help you gain clarity on your goals. Some authors like to sell the workbook, but I think giving it away for free is the perfect way to say **"thank you" to my readers**.

Bonus 2: Free Book - Value 12.95$

Grab a **free short book** with **22+ Techniques for Meditation**. The book will introduce you to a range of meditation practices you can use to help you develop your inner awareness, inner calm, and overall sense of well-being. You will also learn how to begin a meditation practice that works for you regardless of your schedule. These meditation techniques work for everyone, regardless of age or fitness level. Check it out at the link below!

Bonus 3: Free audiobook - Value 14.95$

If you love listening to audiobooks on the go or would enjoy a narration as you read along, I have great news for you. You can download the audiobook version of *my books* for **FREE** just by signing up for a FREE 30-day trial! You can find the audio versions of my books (depending on availability) at the following link.

Join my Review Team!

Are you an avid reader looking to have more insights into spirituality? Do you want to get free books in exchange for an honest review? You can do so by joining my Review Team! You will get priority access to my books before they are released. You only need to follow me on Booksprout, and you will get notified every time a new Review Copy is available for my latest release!

For all the Freebies, visit the following link:

>> https://smartpa.ge/MelissaGomes<<

OR scan the QR Code with your phone's camera.

I'm here because of you

When you're supporting an independent author,
you're supporting a dream. Please leave
an honest review by scanning
the QR code below and clicking on the "Leave a
Review" Button.

★★★★★

https://smartpa.ge/MelissaGomes

Chapter 1: Astrology Fundamentals

In this chapter, we will cover the history of astrology and where it is now. The origins of astrology are shrouded in mystery and dispute, but we will be talking about the oldest form of astrology, in the classical tradition. This includes Western astrology,Vedic and Greek, although our focus will be on the Vedic tradition.

We will talk about Nostradamus' predictions and how accurately they turned out. We'll see how Western astrologers were influenced by Vedic astrology and other Eastern forms of astrology throughout history. The origins of Modern Western astrology are unclear, but we can see that it has a long and important history. Naturally, there are disputes about the origins of Western astrology. We know that the Ancient Greeks used a form of astrology; an Athenian court consulted Plato as an astrologer. This evidence indicates that they used a form of astrology but did not explore it further.

The Magi, or wise men, who came from the east in a caravan with gifts for the Christ child, are thought to have been astrologers. The Persians, Arabs, and Egyptians all had some form of astrology present in their cultures before the Common Era. Astrology, as we know it today, did not become popular in the west until Ptolemy created the Tetrabiblos around 150 CE. It is clear that people knew about planetary positions and had some knowledge of astrology, however,much of it was lost or rewritten hundreds of years after Ptolemy's work.

In 600 BCE, the Babylonians had a method of observing and recording planetary movements, and a cosmological model which related the planets with the stars and zodiac signs; similar to the astrological methods we use today.

Astrology can assist us in living in harmony with nature's elements and cycles; selecting the best time for everything from farming to relationships to work, and engaging in psychological exploration and past life lessons. It can also assist us in healing our disconnect from the natural cycles of the universe. If we want to see a change in our lives, it helps to know what is happening beyond ourselves. Astrology helps us to understand the world and our part in it. It is not fortune-telling but a way of interpreting the omens around us and how these influence our lives.

Over the years, astrological symbolism has been used by people from all walks of life, including scientists, mystics, artists, and even royalty. Today, astronomy is popularly used to explore the solar system's cycles and how it influences life on Earth. In many ways, modern science has come full circle

Astrology is not a new subject; it is older than humanity itself. The cycles and patterns created by the astrological planets are as old as time. The cycles of the solar system repeat at great intervals, and these same cycles appear to have great significance to all of us. Astrology recognizes these cycles and shows how we respond to and interact with them. However, the cycles do not define us or control us. They are there to help us navigate our way through life. The knowledge of the cycles has always been with us, but humans have always looked to find patterns and meaning in the patterns they see around them.

Astrology is primarily based on Fire, Earth, Air, and Water. Every element has a way of interacting with the other 3 elements. When elements come together in extremes, they cause friction, and an uneasy truce can ensue.

Astrology and astronomy work together. The heavenly bodies had their names long before people understood the cycles of the motions of the planets. Early astronomers began tracking these movements, and the cycles of our solar system gradually became better understood. Eventually, the symbolism used by astronomers to refer to the planetary bodies became the modern astrological symbols we use today.

When we see a constellation in the sky, how it looks and certain changes tell us that something is happening there and can give us valuable astronomical information. When we establish patterns of meaning in these constellations, we begin to make updates to the theories about the solar system. There is a relationship between astronomy and astrology that helps guide us in understanding the earth, our solar system, and our place in the universe. Astrologically, the positions of the planets, the number of planets in certain houses of the chart, and other important placements of the planets all suggest that we are not the center of the universe at all, and that we live and move and interact in a much more harmonious universe than we might imagine at first glance.

Today, astrology is practiced by many individuals in many different ways. It is a powerful art and science that can help us understand the cycles of the universe and have an intimate understanding of our own lives. It can help us change our lives for the better and help us to access the immense power of the universe to guide our lives to the right path.

Pythagoras, the ancient Greek philosopher and mathematician, regarded astrology and geometry as equally valid branches of study. The Classic Greek text 'A History of Astronomy' discusses Pythagoras and his early years as a student of geometry and astronomy; he also studied meteorology, geography, and optics.

Astrology came to the forefront during the Renaissance period when Copernicus began to suggest that the Earth was not the center of the universe but instead one planet circling around the sun. This turned the Western world's perception of the sun, moon, and planets upside down.

Despite Copernicus' discoveries, astrology remained popular. Astronomer Johannes Kepler studied both astronomy and astrology, and insisted that you could combine the two sciences. Kepler used astrology to accurately predict the future while he worked to bring astronomy and astrology into proper harmony, advancing the understanding of planetary motion that we know today.

During the Renaissance period, astrology and astronomy were also studied by scientists like Tycho Brahe and Galileo. This renewed interest in astrology lasted throughout the 17th Century into the 18th Century. During this time, the British Empire was growing, and the East India Company was dominating trade. Voyages of exploration during periods that the East India Company had control were recorded in astrological charts, and they consulted the astrologers on board before the company sent their ships out. However, the scientific revolution brought astrology down from its lofty heights.

Astrology and astronomy were linked in Europe through the influential early astronomer Ptolemy, who was the father of astrology. Ptolemy was renowned for his work in astronomy and the method he developed for recording the stars. His work was considered influential for more than two hundred years, and included highly accurate astronomical charts and astronomical positions of the planets.

The energies of the cosmic bodies also work within us, and their movements activate energy within us and the natural world. The more we know about astrology, astronomy, and the larger universe, the more we can know ourselves. We all carry a planet called our "moon" that influences our energy and how we relate to others. Our sun is our heart; it is our inner spirit and soul that we can express to others. Our moon is our unconsciousness, and how we combine those two things affects how we see the world.

Modern western astrology employs the tropical zodiac based on the symbolic relationship between the Earth and the Sun to create a chart for a specific time, date, and location. The eight visible planets' orbs are all included, and the astrological designated genders have been incorporated into the astrological chart. The tropical zodiac runs from the vernal equinox to the following equinox.

Vedic, Chinese, Hellenistic, and Modern Western astrology are among the various astrological disciplines. Each style has its strengths, but shares common symbols. Northern Hemisphere astrologers generally use the tropical system, where the Zodiac signs run clockwise from Aries through to Pisces. In contrast, Eastern Hemisphere astrologers base their charts on the lunar months, like Vedic astrology, and use the 12 signs according to the 12 lunar months consistingof 354 days each year.

Ptolemy, Carl Jung, Alan Leo, Dane Rudhyar, and other historical figures influenced modern astrological practices. Modern astrology studies the energies and influences of the planets and stars on individuals, and astrologers often use astrology as a tool to determine patterns in our lives. Now more than ever, astrology can help us understand our lives and gain more insight into our cycles.

In astronomy, the term "celestial sphere" refers to the universe outside our planet, and to describe the position of the sun and surrounding planets in the sky. Conversely within astrology, "celestial sphere" refers to the sun and sun signs, or the twelve Zodiac signs. These signs follow the cycles of the Earth as the it moves through space during its revolutions around the sun. The twelve zodiac signs also follow a cycle of approximately equal lengths within the zodiac.

The Sumerians in Mesopotamia invented astrology 6,000 years ago, with Vedic astrology dating back 5,000 years in India. Primitive man had a highly developed sense of nature and the cycles that influenced the seasons, the weather, and life in the world, as well as his own life. As sophisticated as the early man was, ancient science differs from what it has become today.

Modern western astrology began with the translation of astrological texts from 1625. The first modern western astrology books were published in Germany and France in 1737 and became very popular readings, especially among the upper classes. However, the interest in astrology subsided during the 1860s as the church gained power, and only revived in the 1920s.

A tropical zodiac is based on the annual cycle of seasons and the tropical year. In ancient times, unlike today, the winter and spring seasons could be interchanged with the fall and summer from time to time. Those seasons began at the spring equinox and ended in fall when the sun again began to rise. The four seasons and the cycle of the tropical year are the basis for a zodiac that moves from spring through fall to spring again without repeating itself in the same order each year.

Only the sun and the eight planets were known during ancient times. At sunset, we know that the sun is descending in the west and getting smaller until it disappears on the horizon. The planets revolve around the sun affecting the Earth, and those planets themselves affect one another. The ancient science of astrology taught the cycles in the heavens are a reflection of the Earth, and the cycles of Earth are reflected in the cycles within nature.

An astrological chart is like a road map that shows us the route we need to take in this life. The planets not only represent us and where we need to go, but they also influence us along a journey toward fulfilling our destiny. A relationship chart shows how the planets affect our relationship with others, whether partners, friends, or family members. An astrological chart can be used as a guide to determine our thinking patterns and guide us in changing our behavior for the better.

The planets leave a footprint in the heavens to describe their dynamic energy inside us, and the natural environment around us. Ancient astrologers named the planets after various gods - believed to be the origin of the planets and the stars. Each planet is related to a zodiac sign, a part of the body or the senses. Planets and signs are assigned genders in the modern world based on the Roman and Greek pantheons, which are firmly patriarchal in nature. However, the planets were seen differently in ancient cultures; the Moon is frequently viewed as the sperm for the Sun's ovum.

We'll be incorporating the theory of sects, an old Hellenistic technique that defined planets as diurnal or nocturnal, meaning day or night. The Sun is considered a daytime celestial body, and the Moon is a nocturnal cosmic object. Planets can be dualities, such as air and water, or primary qualities, such as hot and cool. Planetary interpretation is very subjective. Some people might like their Sun as masculine, for example, and their Moon as feminine, or vice versa. Planetary interpretation can be "right" for you but not necessarily for someone else.

The planetary cycles have seasons, which move at different speeds around the zodiac; every planet operates on the same schedule. As a complete principle, it also ignores the concept of retrograde motion, which changes the cycles completely. The solar system is a living organism that breathes in and out, with each planetary body having both day and night energy.

Chapter 2: The Elements and Modalities

This chapter will discuss the modalities and the four key elements of astrology. We will also discuss the different astrological signs ruled by Mars and their planetary aspects, which will help you better understand your personality and behavior. You should understand your natal chart elements well to understand the Astrological characteristics. Each has energies and traits you will hopefully learn to understand and use to your benefit.

Astrological signs are the constellations of the Zodiac. Every constellation has different characteristics and traits depending on the zodiac sign it belongs to. In every chart, twelve astrological signs are aligned and positioned in the calculation of the birth chart. These signs are the springs of the Zodiac, and their energies, like our moon sign, influence our lives in every possible way. As you will learn, psychological compatibility and how these energies can blend or conflict with each other. These traits characterize an individual's personality and behavior and can help one understand them better in certain situations.

Cardinal Signs

Sun Signs: Aries, Cancer, Libra, and Capricorn

Cardinal signs enjoy starting new projects but may lack the perseverance to see them through. They're quick to go off on tangents and enjoy getting involved in multiple projects at once. The second element of Astrology is the Water element.

Fixed Signs

Sun Signs: Taurus, Leo, Scorpio, and Aquarius

Fixed signs are dependable and prefer to finish what they start, but sometimes have trouble starting something new because they like to develop an idea more thoroughly before committing to it.. They tend to focus more on career and financial stability than other signs. Take Aquarius, for example; Aquarians are known to be practical decision-makers and are very organized in their approach to life. They are also known for their detached personalities and tend to focus less on emotions than some of the other signs.

Mutable Signs

Sun Signs: Gemini, Virgo, Sagittarius, and Pisces

Mutable signs like to get ideas off the ground and could be known for jumping from one idea to another throughout their lives. They dislike routine and may find it hard to move forward with projects that aren't flexible. Mutable signs are also indecisive and dislike making decisions. They may find it difficult to commit to projects or people because they have no clear vision to follow. Mutable signs can also be prone to random mood swings and may become overly emotional in certain situations.

Elements in the Zodiac

Elements are the Zodiac's most important aspects of your personality. They affect your behavior and how you deal with things daily. Each Zodiac sign is linked to an element or archetype. There are four elements, and each represents a particular trait a Zodiac sign can have. Some signs of the Zodiac are ruled by more than one element, with more than one ruling planet, and vice versa. The elements represent the four kinds of energy that influence people and things; Earth, Air, Water and Fire These elements can transform into one another during different situations and are represented by the four basic elements that make up our world.

The elements represent archetypal characteristics within a person and interact with one another. The four elements are also connected to various zodiac signs due to their corresponding qualities. This section will discuss each element individually, along with the personality characteristics those signs possess.

Fire

Fire is the energy of transformation, action, and of the day. The Sun provides the heat and light required to survive, and Fire is both heat and movement. We can harness the Fire energy of the planets to empower our will to move relations forward. Fire also represents our ability to lead and forge a path forward. It is represented in many mythologies, most notably in the story of the Phoenix - a mythical bird that rebirths itself by burning and then rising again from its ashes. Zodiac signs that embody the element of Fire are Aries, Leo, and Sagittarius.

Air

Air is the energy of communication and intellect; it surrounds us and connects all living things. Air is related to both thought and the mind, and seeks to know universal truths through observation and wisdom. Air also has the power to influence other people's thoughts and feelings; as such, some truths can change opinions or minds and draw people together for a cause or belief, like the truth that people will share with others. Air also represents the ability to relate to and connect with other people outside our immediate circle. Discord and chaos are also formed through the air, as the emotion is felt through jealousy, frustration, and confusion over plans changing. Gemini, Libra, and Aquarius are zodiac signs that belong to the element of Air.

Water

Water is the energy of emotions and the subconscious; it is the element that connects the spiritual and physical planes by revealing feelings and emotions. Water is related to heart energy and its role in our actions and relationships. It can manifest as tears or rivers; the connecting force brings life to the elements. Water corresponds to the flow of our emotions and the subconscious mind. Water signs are highly intuitive and psychic and often have the power to communicate with spirits and ghosts. Water is similar to Air in that it signifies the movement of things. Cancer, Scorpio, and Pisces are Zodiac signs under the element of Water.

Earth

Earth is the energy of endurance and growth; it is the substance of our bodies and the expression of our innermost natures. Earth represents the five senses and the material world. Earth rules the senses of touch and taste and gives us a body to embody our unique natures. Earth also relates to our ability to grow and change as we age and experience life. Earth corresponds to our drive to survive and is often used to characterize the importance associated with material possessions. Taurus, Virgo, and Capricorn are Zodiac signs under the Earth element.

Chapter 3: The Sun Signs

This chapter will go over the twelve sun signs of the zodiac and how they affect us. We will also discuss dualities and some interesting facts about each sign. Signs or constellations appear in the sky, some of which are visible in the Northern Hemisphere and others in the Southern Hemisphere. There are twelve constellations, each representing a Greek god or goddess. When looked up on a map, these constellations are the signs of the zodiac.

The ancients believed that the sun travels through these constellations each month, and these signs change through the year to represent the sun's transition across the sky. The Babylonians observed these constellations and used astrological readings to discover when certain events happened or what would happen in the immediate future. This knowledge became popularized in ancient Greece and was used to help people with their daily lives, as well as to help them in the areas of finances and relationships.

The twelve sun signs or zodiac signs have had various interpretations throughout history. They each represent characteristics and traits which can be seen in the people born under the sign of that constellation. Each sign has a different meaning, depending on the period or culture when people observed them.

Each sign represents a month, so the month you were born determines which sun sign you are under the Babylonian system. If you are born in January, you are Capricorn. Today, your sign is determined by the day of your birth, not the month.

Aries

The first sign of the zodiac is Aries, which rules the first house in the horoscope. People born under this sign are usually confident and courageous but can also be hot-headed. Under Aries, people tend to be ambitious but reckless. Aries is a Mars-ruled, day cardinal, Fire sign that represents youth. It opposes Libra, an Air sign, and governs the head and eyes. This is a dynamic, pioneering sign regarded as a leader by others, as such they may have an aggressive and reactionary personality. A planet in the sign of Aries will give this temperament a boost.

People born under Aries are natural-born leaders and shine in many careers. They are considered multi-talented and are often gifted with keen intellects. They are quick thinkers who can solve problems and develop new ideas. However, if Mercury is in conjunction with Jupiter or Saturn in the sign of Aries, the person will become very lazy and irritable.

Taurus

The second sign of the zodiac is Taurus, which rules the second house in the horoscope. People born under this sign are usually stubborn and passionate about their work. Both the Sun and Moon are in Taurus, which means that people may behave like a bull or charge into situations. Taurus is a Venus-ruled day Earth sign that represents maturity. It is in trine to Virgo, and is a fixed sign that is considered stubborn in nature. They are extremely determined and boldly act when getting things done. If Mercury is in conjunction with Aries, they will break through all barriers that try to keep them from the stage of life when you realize you have a connection to the physical world. Taurus is associated with the throat and vocal cords, and the metal is copper. This sign is sensual, practical, and loyal but can also be stubborn and materialistic.

Gemini

Gemini is a mutable Air sign that rules the day, and is ruled by Mercury in his mind/messenger incarnation. Yellow stones benefit Gemini's chest, lungs, nervous system, arms, and shoulders. Gemini rules communication and intellectual pursuits; this sign is talkative, energetic, chatty, and craves companionship. Gemini is also an Air sign that rules the third and fourth houses of the horoscope.

Gemini is a dual sign that represents a balance between strategy and communication. They can talk their way into just about anything, and their communication skills are highly developed. Jupiter makes Gemini focused and determined so they can accomplish all their goals. This sign is known for clever inventions and inventions in technology. They have strong mental stability and are adept at seeing both sides of an issue and exploring different possibilities.

Cancer

Cancer represents another dual sign. This sign is governed by its ruling planet, the Moon, and rules both the day and the night. Cancer is associated with the Water element. People born under this sign are known for their sensitivity, emotional depth, creativity, and intuition. The Moon affects this sign strongly, as Cancer is represented by The Crab, a night cardinal Water sign. Capricorn, the Earth sign, is its polarity, making it very sensitive and emotional.

Cancers are known as nurturers and have deep compassion for others. They tend to have complex emotions and are often touchy-feely individuals. Cancer will become very jealous and possessive if Mars is in conjunction with Libra.

Leo

Leo is a fixed Fire sign that governs the minutes and hours in the body. People born with Leo as their Sun sign are often dramatic and outgoing but can also be self-centered and domineering. Its metal is gold, and its lucky gemstones are amber and tiger's eye. Leos are born leaders; magnetic and affectionate. They are self-assured and dynamic, and they carry the Sun's radiance within them. Leos are ambitious and driven to achieve all their desires. They are natural-born leaders and love to be in charge and lead others. If Jupiter is with Mercury or the Sun in Leo, they will often become dramatic or selfish in their approach to life.

Virgo

Virgo is a night-mutable Earth sign ruled by Mercury and symbolized by the maiden or virgin, which means "whole unto herself." Virgos are detail-oriented and analytical but can fall into servitude rather than service and forget to take care of themselves.. The crowd and the multitude are symbolic of this sign. Virgo governs the sixth house in the horoscope. This sign is associated with the feet and toes and governs health and healing. From this position in the body, Virgo governs the ankles, knees, toes and fingertips in gout and arthritis.

Libra

Libra is a cardinal Air sign of the day ruled by Venus in her more cerebral incarnation. They are fair, peaceful, creative, and strive to achieve a harmonious balance in everything they do. Libra governs the seventh house in the horoscope. While Libra is a sign concerned with relationships, it is one that also has strong personal ideals and independent natures. Libra is associated with and symbolized by a pair of scales. Libra governs the throat and mouth and is associated with a marital relationship or with the upkeep and growth of a family.

Scorpio

Scorpio is a cardinal Water sign that rules the night and is ruled by modern Pluto and traditional Mars. It rules the reproductive system and sexual organs and is associated with the scorpion, serpent, and phoenix. Scorpio governs the eighth8th house in the horoscope, which symbolizes the extremes of life, death, and the unconscious mind. Scorpio is associated with the Warrior archetype and symbolizes the conflict between the public persona and the private self. . It has a fixed quality, which lends to the intensity and tenacity of the sign.

Sagittarius

Sagittarius is a day mutable Fire sign, ruled by Jupiter, that represents the archer. It is in charge of the hips, thighs, and liver. This sign is a wanderer who enjoys all forms of exploration. They have a spiritual bent, are visionary, and can see the big picture of life. It has a very strong and independent nature and is adventurous and extroverted. Sagittarius rules the ninthhouse in the horoscope, which is associated with higher education and travel.

Capricorn

Capricorn is a night cardinal Earthsign that rules the skeleton, teeth, and joints. Capricorns are determined to climb the ladder of success, but the expectations of others may influence them. This sign is often viewed as one of the most ambitious signs of the zodiac because Capricorn has a fixed quality. They can be very stubborn if what they want falls outside their boundaries. This sign is associated with the goat and crossing the sea of troubles. Capricorn governs the tenth house in the horoscope, symbolizing leadership, achievement, and power.

Aquarius

Aquarius is another Air sign of the day and is associated with the "water bearer" or the "pourer." It is ruled by Uranus and governs the shoulders and arms. Aquarius has an interest in humanitarian causes and trends. People born under Aquarius are often regarded as eccentric and detached individuals. This sign is associated with lead and the gemstones obsidian and sapphire, and people under this sign are creative and committed to causes. Still, they can also be emotionally distant and anarchistic at times.

Pisces

Pisces is a mutable Water sign that rules the feet, lymphatic system, and third eye at night. They are highly sensitive, creative, and mystical beings who frequently struggle with boundaries and can become victims or martyrs. Pisces is a water sign that governs the twelfth house in the horoscope, which in mythology is associated with the sea, underworld, and death. It is governed by Neptune, the planet of illusion and delusion.

Chapter 4: Ascendant Signs and Decans

This chapter goes over the zodiac's twelve rising signs, their corresponding negative traits, and how to deal with them. For the spellcaster, the natural signs are of utmost importance. The zodiac is a chain of twelve signs shaping certain personality traits in an individual that correlate with the signs they are under.

The ascendant represents the conditioning brought about by your birth and early childhood and is the most visible aspect of a person when they show up in the world. These traits are then further reinforced by education, culture, and other influences throughout life.

To calculate your rising sign accurately, you must know your birth time. If you do not know the time you were born, you can go to the nearest city with a hospital that records the time of birth or use an online astrology calculator found online.

Each sign has a positive and negative side, ruled by its planets or celestial bodies. However, the negative traits are not universal and are not always present when the signs of the horoscope are rising. Put more bluntly: not everyone is an asshole, just as not everyone has Venus in the sign of Capricorn. Some signs are more adaptive than others and can take another trait and make it their own, while others cannot and tend to fall towards the negative aspects of their sign.

Aries

The Aries are linear, fearless, and impulsive. However, those traits tend to make Aries self-centered without common social graces. They can also be limited in resources and at the mercy of their circumstances which can bring about some adversity.

Traits: Courageous, Stubborn, Adventurous, Energetic, Positive

Negative Traits: Impatient, Domineering, Self-centered, Impulsive, Reckless

Aries is a cardinal sign, and those born with this sign are active and direct. They are typically quick on their feet and drawn to sports and competitive activities, though their competitiveness is frequently self-directed. They do not like to be idle but get bored easily and must challenge themselves to keep up their energy. To do so, they often have to get worked up and exert both effort and willpower. Aries are generally bold and brave but sometimes become reckless in their attempts to avoid danger. Their impetuousness can land them in dangerous situations. Aries can be overbearing towards others. Their assertiveness can often land them in hot water when they do not practice temperance. Aries can be self-centered, but most of the time, they are self-determined. Aries often choose a path of action over thought.

Aries is ruled by the planet Mars which gives them energy in an individualistic way. This energy gives them confidence, courage, and optimism. It's an instinctual drive that tells them to go for it. However, this energy can sometimes get out of control. Aries can also be headstrong, impatient, ambitious, and assertive, making them pushy. They may end up hurting themselves or others in their attempts to avoid danger or challenge themselves. Aries can be resentful when their attempts to avoid danger fail and become vulnerable.

Conflict with Aries arises when they find themselves doing or saying what they want rather than considering others' needs. Aries is ruled by Mars and has Venus in Aries, and is thus conceited in her abilities and appearance, and those traits need to be kept in check. Conflict with Libra arises when Libra looks for relationships to validate who they are. In contrast, Aries is still looking for validation from others and sees what they want to offer as real validation.

Taurus

The Taurus rising sign is a strong, solid tree that is pleasant to be around unless pushed. They are devoted and enjoy pleasant smells, tastes, sounds, and touches. They may also have a pleasant voice.

Traits: Quiet, Receptive, Stable, Patient, Earthy, Practical

Negative Traits: Sensitive, Moody, Stubborn, Fond of Comfort, Lazy

Taurus is a fixed sign. Being ruled by Venus makes those born under this rising sign very sensual. They are focused on pleasing themselves and others with pleasant experiences such as food, touch, music, and activity. They are patient and enjoy simple pleasures. Their senses can be activated easily by anything pleasant or pleasurable. Their senses of touch and smell are very strong. The Taurus is composed and calm; they can remain calm in stressful situations and seek solutions patiently. However, they are very slow to warm up to new or hard situations and dislike conflict. They can be dependent on others and are slow to do anything, which puts them in danger of losing this physical comfort. When they are threatened or harmed in some way, they lose confidence and become more stubborn or helpless.

Taurus is ruled by Venus, the planet of beauty, love, and romance. Those born under this sign are generally friendly, faithful, generous, sensual, brave, patient, and consistent. They are good at maintaining healthy relationships and love to provide beautiful experiences for others. They are loyal and rarely betray confidence. Taurus needs more self-confidence to fend off negative influences. When they feel threatened, they become more timid and dependent.

Gemini

Individuals born under the sign of Gemini are both social and chaotic. They are endlessly curious, witty, and a joy to be around in a social setting, but their attention spans are short, so expect them to move on quickly.

Traits: Curious, Witty, Social, Flexible, Talkative

Negative traits: Conflicted, Unfocused, Distracted, Hyperactive

Gemini is a mutable sign and is governed by the planet Mercury. Those born under this sign are quick, adaptable, and curious, with logic and words mindlessly. They enjoy intellectual conversation but are distracted easily. Thus they are good for parties or crowds where they can keep their focus but change interests frequently. Gemini can be restless and unfocused and do better in environments that allow them to exchange ideas. Their quick minds make them good at communication. Gemini has the gift of gab and is very skilled in social interaction. They are restless and have no trouble grasping new social trends or philosophical ideas. They're usually able to adapt to new environments and people quickly but often have trouble staying focused on one thing for a long. Gemini's wandering minds keep them from being grounded, and their flights of fancy keep others amused. Gemini has an unpredictable mind and can change very quickly.

Cancer

Individuals born with Cancer signs are sensitive and loving souls, but when their mood is low, they can be moody and needy. When they are stressed, they may gain weight and have digestive problems.

Traits: Sensitive, Loving, Homebody, Moody

Negative traits: Emotional, Crabby, Resentful, Overprotective

Cancer is a cardinal sign and is dominated by the Moon. People born under this sign are generally sensitive, sympathetic, and loving individuals. People born under this sign enjoy spending time with loved ones and being home where they can feel safe and secure. They seek the approval of others and are generally gentle and considerate. They are dedicated and loyal. When stressed, Cancer can become anxious, self-conscious, and moody. Because of their insecurity, Cancer can become overprotective or clingy. Cancer needs a safe emotional base to thrive and express its nurturing side effectively. The negative side to this sign is sensitivity which causes them to become anxious and dependent on their emotional security.

Leo

Leos are king and queen of the jungle, strong leaders who are ambitious and determined to succeed. They tend to have a good sense of direction in life.

Traits: Ambitious, Leader, Self-Centered, Dominant, Active

Negative traits: Arrogant, Stubborn, Bossy, Obnoxious

Leo is a fixed sign. People born under this sign are magnetic, with lion's mane hair and a sunny round face. They are dramatic and demonstrative, and they crave attention. However, they can become bossy and throw tantrums if they do not receive it. As the center of our solar system, the Sun represents the Leo-rising individual who believes that the world revolves around them. They are dramatic and demonstrative and tell it like it is. Leo is ruled by the Sun. They are known for being energetic, passionate, and radiant. They love to be the center of attention and tend to care very little about what others think of them. They are confident and optimistic but can easily get offended when feeling threatened. They are also known as "the light bearers" for their ability to shine a light on things important to themselves and others. They are natural-born leaders with an ability that inspires confidence in others.

Virgo

Virgo-rising people are the zodiac's analysts and worriers, and they are usually neatly dressed and appear a little uptight. They are typically shy, but they warm up as you get to know them.

Traits: Analytical, Organized, Nervous, Perfectionist

Negative traits: Boring, Self-Centered, Micro-manager

Virgo is a mutable sign and is under Mercury's rule. People born in this sign are analytical, intelligent, and practical. They live with their heads in the clouds and their feet on the ground. They tend to be nervous but are not swayed by their emotions. They prefer to be organized and managed, but it rarely happens. Virgo-Aries individuals have a talent for learning quickly. Virgo is represented by the planet Mercury which can change the sign's energy depending on its position.

Libra

Individuals born under the sign of Libra are charming and enjoy interacting with others. They can, however, have a passive-aggressive streak because they are constantly attempting to balance those Libra scales by looking at all sides. If you find yourself dealing with one of these people, do not be surprised if you see them flitting from one person to another at an inconvenient time.

Traits: Charming, Fair-minded, Diplomatic, Flirty, Social

Negative traits: Pessimistic, Passive-Aggressive, Dependent

Venus and any planets close to the ascendant rule Libra rising. Libra is a cardinal sign and is ruled by the planet Venus. This sign represents people who are charming and social. Libra natives typically enjoy interacting with others and are very aware of people's moods. They can be indecisive due to this fine balancing act between calmness and drama. Librans dislike confrontation and only change their ways when they have to. In love, they are usually sexy and possessive. This may be a weakness for some Librans, but in others, this is their inner strength. They focus on relationships and seek balance within them.

Scorpio

Scorpio's rising signs are magnetic, intimidating, and intense. They are very private and secretive about their inner lives, but they have great power and are passionate and creative in everything they do.

Traits: Intense, Passionate, Magnetic, Secretive, Self-Sufficient

Negative traits: Manipulative, Self-Destructive, Jealous, Stingy

Pluto and Mars, the ruling planets of Scorpio-rising people, will alter the influence of the rising sign. Pluto's energy is very destructive and power-oriented. Scorpio natives have strong instincts and are suspicious, secretive, and intense. Scorpio's intense energy often makes them appear intimidating and secretive. People born under this sign are clever, passionate, and driven to succeed. They prefer to be alone and tend to be self-righteous or suspicious. They are often manipulative or quick to anger when they are threatened.

Sagittarius

Sagittarius-rising people enjoy the freedom and have a large library or many books beside their beds. They are also perceived as naive, but their likeability and sense of humor often keep them out of trouble.

Traits: Outgoing, Witty, Optimistic, Open-minded

Negative traits: Lazy, Disobedient, Indifferent, Overbearing

Sagittarius is a Fire sign ruled by the planet Jupiter. People born under Sagittarius are intellectual and enjoy discussing their ideas and knowledge with others. They are optimistic and curious and prefer to live and let live. They are eager to learn and have a desire to travel. They are honest, unselfish, and generous. Sagittarians usually express these traits because they seek popularity and love to be free and independent. They do not like taking orders from others and dislike being tied down.

Capricorn

Capricorns are ambitious and work-oriented, but their serious demeanor can make them emotionally cold. They value security and the ability to provide for their families and partners, but they are also concerned about not being or doing enough.

Traits: Ambitious, Responsible, Dependable, Practical

Negative traits: Aloof, Calculating, Materialistic

Capricorn is an Earth sign ruled by the planet Saturn. Those born under this sign prefer practicality to sentimentality and are often aloof about their emotions. They want to succeed and are responsible and dependable. Capricorn people dislike showing affection, making commitments, or losing control. They are cautious about their safety but also enjoy material comforts and security.

Aquarius

Aquarius rising people are quirky, curious, and a little rebellious. They are friendly, enjoy a good intellectual debate, and can be emotionally detached while caring about the world as activists.

Traits: Curious, Original, Intellectual, Artistic, Rebellious

Negative traits: Flirty, Unreliable, Unemotional, Inflexible

The moon-ruled sign of Aquarius is the ray of intelligence and creativity. Aquarius natives usually have a mind that never stops thinking or questioning. They are original and inventive and love to think for themselves. They are people who will rebel if it means going against the system. They are energetic and frank. In love, they strive for equality and independence because they find traditional understandings and relationships boring and suffocating.

Pisces

Pisces-rising people are dreamers, compassionate, and often have a shape-shifting quality that mirrors those around them.

They are vulnerable to manipulation and may be susceptible to prescribed drugs.

Traits: Creative, Dreamer, Compassionate, Mystical

Negative traits: Solipsistic, Maladjusted, Dependent, Preoccupied, Vulnerable to Manipulation

Neptune rules Pisces rising, and planets near the ascendant influence it. Neptune rules deep waters but also drug and alcohol abuse. Neptune brings out emotions and fantasies; people may not know how to filter them. Pisces-rising people are often misunderstood because they are dreamers who deal in fantasy and wishy-washy. As a result, they may be self-centered and can seem undependable. They are compassionate and often empathetic. Pisceans like to keep its options open and avoid making long-term commitments.

Decans

In the first century CE, the Egyptian stars were combined with the twelve signs of the zodiac to form the decan system. The decans symbolize a 1/12th part of the zodiac based on their position along the ecliptic. Astrologers use the decans to interpret the influences of a person's horoscope when the moon is full or new in a sign.

The complete decan list begins with the first decan on the Eastern horizon of the zodiac and ends with the 10th decan on the western horizon of the zodiac. Decans are used to emphasize specific sign combinations and planets in the horoscope.

The following list contains the first seven decans from East to West. Each decan is separated by the diagram you see above. The first decan represents the first 30 degrees of a sign, the second decan represents the next 30 degrees, and so on to the last decan's 30 degrees.

March 21 to April 19: Aries

Because Mars rules Aries, the planet of action, energy, passion, and aggression, it amplifies the already fiery Aries. As a result, those born under the sign of Aries are self-assured, competitive, ambitious, independent, and a little combative.

Mars rules the Aries decan from March 21 to March 30. As a result, people born on these dates will exhibit typical Aries characteristics.

The Sun is the secondary ruler of the Leo decan from March 30 to April 9. Individuals born in this decan will exhibit sun-ruled characteristics in addition to their primary Aries/Mars traits. They may enjoy being the center of attention and be more creative than other Aries.

Jupiter is the secondary ruler of the Sagittarius decan from April 10 to April 19. As a result, someone born in this decan may be more adventurous than other Aries and more philosophical, open, and optimistic.

April 20 to May 20: Taurus

Venus, the planet of love, sensual pleasure, and decadence rule Taurus. As a result, typical Tauruses are interested in aesthetics and enjoy engaging their senses as much as possible. They may also be obsessed with the finer things in life.

The Taurus decan, which runs from April 20 to April 29, is ruled by Venus. People born in this decan will thus present as typical Tauruses.

Mercury is the secondary ruler of the Virgo decan from April 30 to May 9. Individuals born under this second decan are likely to be even more communicative than the average Taurus. They could also be more intelligent.

Saturn is the third ruler of the Taurus decan from May 10 to May 19. As a result, these third-decan Taurus may be more responsible and hardworking than typical.

May 21 to June 20: Gemini

Mercury, the planet of communication and intellect, rules Gemini. As a result, Geminis are social, curious, quick-witted, and knowledgeable.

Mercury rules the Gemini decan from May 21 to May 30. Those born in this decan will exhibit typical Gemini characteristics.

Venus is the secondary ruler of the Gemini decan from May 31 to June 9. Geminis born in the second decan are more sensual and tactile than others.

Uranus is the third ruler of the Gemini decan from June 10 to June 20. Individuals born in this decan will be more self-sufficient, rebellious, and innovative than other Geminis.

June 21 to July 22: Cancer

Cancer is ruled by the Moon, which governs both human emotion and emotional comfort. As a result, Cancers are sensitive, intuitive, nurturing, deep, and sometimes mercurial.

The Moon rules Cancer from July 21 to June 30. People born in the first decan will exhibit typical Cancer characteristics.

Pluto is the secondary ruler of the Cancer decan from July 1 to July 10. People born in this decan will be more intense and inwardly focused than other Cancers.

Neptune is the third ruler of the Cancer decan from July 11 to July 22. People born in this decan will be more creative and spiritual than other Cancers.

July 23 to August 22: Leo

The Sun rules Leo, bringing warmth, radiance, and attention to the sign. As a result, Leos tend to light up every room they enter and enjoy widespread popularity—and the confidence that comes with it. They are also extremely energetic and can create a whirlwind environment around themselves.

The Sun rules the Leo decan from July 23 to August 1. People born in this decan will exhibit typical Leo characteristics.

Jupiter is the secondary ruler of the Leo decan from August 2 to August 11. People born in this decan are brighter than typical Leos and enjoy taking their group on an adventure.

Mars is the third ruler of the Leo decan from August 12 to August 22. Those born in this decan will be more explosive and aggressive than the average Leo, for their sun can instantly turn to fire.

August 23 to September 22: Virgo

Mercury, the planet of communication and intellect, rules Virgo. The latter trait is more emphasized in Virgos, who are deep thinkers. Mercury also influences Virgos to be well-organized, detail-oriented, and punctual.

Mercury rules the Virgo decan from August 23 to September 1. Individuals born under this decan will appear to be typical Virgos.

Saturn is the secondary ruler of the Virgo decan from September 2 to September 11. This means that Virgos born in the second decan are likely to be more determined and hardworking than other Virgos.

Venus is the third ruler of Virgo from September 12 to September 22. As a result, those born in the third decan may be more sensitive to aesthetics than others of their sign.

September 23 to October 22: Libra

Venus, the planet of love and sensual pleasure, rules Libra. The former is emphasized in Libras, who are highly romantic but also have an interest in and talent for aesthetics.

The Libra decan, which runs from September 23 to October 2, is ruled by Venus. People born in this decan will exhibit typical Libra characteristics.

Uranus is the secondary ruler of the Libra decan from October 3 to October 12. This means that Libras born in the second decan may be more interested in expanding their consciousness via astrology, for example, than other Libras. They might also be more creative.

Mercury is the third ruler of the Libra decan from October 13 to October 22. These Libras will then be effective and active communicators.

October 23 to November 21: Scorpio

Pluto, the planet of darkness and mystery, rules Scorpio. As a result, those born under this sign are intense, enigmatic, calculating, passionate, and seductive.

Scorpio is ruled by Pluto and runs from October 23 to November 1. Scorpios born in the first decan will exhibit typical characteristics.

Neptune is the secondary ruler of the Scorpio decan from November 2 to November 11. Individuals born within this second decon will be more imaginative and creative than other Scorpios and less grounded.

The Moon is the third ruler of the Scorpio decan from November 12 to November 21. These Scorpios are more sensitive than others and are also excellent caregivers.

November 22 to December 21: Sagittarius

Jupiter, the planet of fortune and adventure, rules Sagittarius. As a result, people born under this sign are optimistic, free-spirited, and always looking for new experiences.

A Sagittarius decan, ruled by Jupiter, runs from November 22 to December 1. People born in this decan will exhibit typical Sagittarius characteristics.

Mars is the secondary ruler of the Sagittarius decan from December 2 to December 11. Those born under this decan will be more fiery and confident than others of their sign.

The Sun is the third ruler of the Sagittarius decan from December 12 to December 21. People born in the third decan may be more energetic, charismatic, and self-centered than others in their sign.

December 22 to January 19: Capricorn

Saturn, the planet of discipline, hard work, and ambition, rules Capricorn. Capricorns are, as a result, all of those things: hardworking, disciplined, and ambitious. They live to crush even the most difficult targets.

Saturn rules the Capricorn decan from December 22 to December 31. Those born in the first decan will exhibit typical Capricorn characteristics.

Venus is the secondary ruler of the Capricorn decan from January 1 to January 10. People born under this decan are more sensual and romantic than typical Capricorns. They may be prone to fantasizing and seeking decadence wherever they can find it.

Mercury is the third ruler of the Capricorn decan from January 11 to January 19. Capricorns focus their ambitions and efforts on intellectual pursuits.

January 20 to February 18: Aquarius

Uranus, the planet of individuality and radicalism, rules Aquarius. Those born under this sign are often ahead of their time, extremely innovative, and slightly eccentric.

The Aquarius decan, which runs from January 20 to January 29, is ruled by Uranus. Those born in this first decan will exhibit typical Aquarius characteristics.

Mercury is the secondary ruler of Aquarius from January 30 to February 8. As a result, second-decan Aquariansare more intellectual and chatty than other Aquariuses.

Venus is the secondary ruler of the Aquarius decan from February 9 to February 18. As a result, people born within this decan may be more interested in the pleasures of life, including love, than other Aquarians.

February 19 to March 20: Pisces

Neptune, the planet of imagination and spirituality, rules Pisces. Pisces people are, therefore, creative, intuitive, and emotionally intense. They are usually on or seeking a spiritual path.

The first decan of Pisces, ruled by Neptune, runs from February 19 to February 28. Those born within this decan will exhibit typical Pisces characteristics.

The Moon is the secondary ruler of the Pisces decan from March 1 to March 10. These Pisces will be even more sensitive than their Pisces counterparts.

Pluto is the third ruler of the Pisces decan from March 11 to March 20. Those born under this decan will be more secretive, mysterious, and cunning than the average Pisces.

Chapter 5: The Planets and Other Celestial Bodies

Planets and other celestial bodies can affect your personality and outlook in life, according to astrology. Here, you will learn which positions are best suited to signs and how to make the best of your birth chart.

Astrology is not about predicting the future with 100% accuracy. It also isn't about fooling people into believing everything is based on luck or destiny. Accurate astrology relies on using fundamental scientific principles and correct calculations to derive the planetary position at the time of a person's birth and then working from there to map the person's character and predict future outcomes. While it is impossible to accurately predict specific events like death, a horoscope offers perspective, particularly when going on a negative course in life.

Sun

The Sun is the primary organizing principle for the solar system and the self. It is a masculine energy that rules the sign of Leo and the heart. Aquarius' Solar Return occurs in August, which gives it a more positive outlook than it usually exhibits during the rest of the year since it will have two retrograde periods. The Sun helps examine old beliefs and patterns of behavior, and its placement in Aquarius will offer a peak into the sign's personality, hopes, and wishes.

The Sun's energy can be both benevolent and egotistical. Other placements can also dull or block it. This includes planets in retrograde motion or squaring, thereby lowering their vibration. For example, Venus in Aries can blind a person to the destructive nature of their ego, and the Sun in Aries can also make a person foolish. On the other hand, a Pisces Sun and a Taurus Moon combination can give a person a spiritual balance that applies to all aspects of life, helping one live by the principles of the heart and not just by ego-driven desires.

The Sun has hidden traits, such as magnetism and charisma. These traits can be blocked or elevated throughout its orbit, giving it a variable quality. Fortunately, there is some control over these traits, and people can learn to harness them as other astrological placements wield them.

Moon

The Moon symbolizes our emotional needs and our relationship with emotions. It is receptive and reflective, emitting no light of its own, and represents the night when we exhale, rest, and recharge our energy. It is also feminine and rules Cancer and the ocean. Most people do not like their moon sign or the ruling planet, but Cancer signs like their ruling planet, the Moon, because they are emotional, strong, adaptable, intuitive, sympathetic, empathetic, and protective: traits that come in handy in a complex world.

Not everyone is comfortable with their moon sign, though. Aries Moons dislike being shy and retiring, while Aquarian Moons hate being pulled in by others. The Moon can be weakened by planets like Saturn, which lowers its vibration and blocks its energy. Even so, the Moon is influenced by Jupiter and Mars, which gives it a positive outlook. Another significant aspect of the moon's position is that it moves through the house of neighbors; hence, it ushers in a new acquaintance when it changes signs.

Mercury

Mercury is a planet that rules Gemini, the twins' sign, and Virgo, the service sign. Mercury is the communicator and represents how we think out a problem and communicate it to others while assisting with problem-solving. Gemini natives have multiple personality disorders due to many influences on their brains. Virgo natives are grounded and practical. They are serious about work and believe in gaining knowledge through experience. Rarely angry, Virgos are prone to worry a lot in Gemini. Mercury also rules Virgo houses that determine employment and finance, and placement in this sign offers an employer's perspective.

Mercury is the messenger of the gods, and it travels near the Sun. It is also linked to the trickster archetype and retrograde three to four times yearly. Retrograde Mercury periods are bad times for making major decisions but offer a good time to brush up on skills since repetition is important to learn from our mistakes. Mercury's ability to travel in retrograde motion illustrates how the information is intentionally distorted. Pisces' planetary return occurs in February, so Sun and Mercury will work harmoniously, thereby giving this sign a more optimistic outlook. This can be viewed negatively in August when Sun and Mercury are in conjunction, or one sign away, from opposition and Mercury, goes direct, resulting in an erratic mindset.

Venus

Venus is the planet of love and femininity in modern astrology. In Greek mythology, it was referred to as Aphrodite. It rules the sign of Libra, governs the heart, and affects our bond with others and sex appeal. Scientists named the planet after a goddess of love. Very rarely does the feminine energy overpower the masculine energy when it comes to planets because their orbits are near one, such as the Sun, Mars, and Mercury, creating subtle vibrations that increase their synergy. Still, newly formed planets like Venus are far from the sun and have no resonance with their masculine energy.

Venus has a cycle that reflects more complex energy, and it is a good idea to consider sign and house placement and aspects of other planets. Libra Venus is romantic and seeks equality in love, which is not always possible. It often conflicts with its ruling planet because it promotes balance, yet it does not understand why ideas are rejected. This planet helps determine your desires in life and makes you susceptible to affection, lust, and jealousy. A Venus placement in humans can also reflect your inner relationships, helping you seek beauty and harmony in life and with others around you.

Mars

In Greek and Roman mythology, Mars is a malefic planet associated with the warrior, athlete, and competitor. It rules Aries, the ram sign, and is a call to action. Mars is the activator of action in the chart, which reminds us to use skills to achieve our aims, overcome obstacles, and prepare for battle since battle is inevitable. Mars often rules Aries, and controls competition and brute force.

Mars has fierce energy and is naturally dualistic; hence, it has difficulty blending with the other forces in the chart. This deficiency results in aggressive and intense behavior. It can also result in physical ailments like skin rashes. Still, it is usually associated with problems caused by overbearing masculine energy that compensates for the lack of feminine energy and can become impulsive and rash.

Jupiter

Jupiter is the first social planet, marking a transition from the personal planets to the more recently discovered outer, transpersonal, or collective planets. Jupiter is the planet of expansion, opportunity, and growth, and it rules Sagittarius, the archer's sign, and the 12th house dealing with hope and transformation. Jupiter is masculine energy associated with heavier planets, and its placement in a sign can accentuate or temper its beauty and value.

Jupiter's tendency to feel lucky increases the likelihood of making poor financial or professional moves; hence, this placement is often a test of one's integrity. One should either overcome this placement's weakness or look for work he is qualified to handle; this is true of Jupiter in Scorpio, which is usually associated with alchemy and mystery, as these qualities heighten intuition and help focus one's energy.

Saturn

Saturn is the second social planet and the last of the original visible to the naked eye planets used in traditional astrology. It rules the Capricorn yin earth sign and represents external authority, boundaries, rules, limitations, fear, denial, and control. It rules Capricorn, the goat's sign, and the 10th house that deals with career and reputation. Although it exhibits a psychological preference toward control and order, this planet has no empathy as it controls through fear.

It therefore negatively interacts with other planets, and transits can result in losses and setbacks.

Uranus

In Astrology, Uranus is an inventive genius who will defy convention and go his own way. This planet represents awakening energy and shattered boundaries. It rules Aquarius, the water bearer's sign, and the 11th house dealing with individuality and friendships. Aquarius is eccentric and rules over the 11th house, which represents our friendships and relationships with friends, co-workers, and others.

Uranus is not a social planet like this one since it rules Aquarius, the eccentric ruler over the 11th house that deals with friendship, relationships, and other individuals. This placement often rules their interactions with others. Uranus is a sign that can break free and seek inner truth, and this planet in your chart shows an individual's potential to break free of those societal and cultural norms. Still, it cannot live without other forces, and transits reveal underlying mental fears.

Neptune

Neptune represents illusion, confusion, consciousness, psychic sensitivity, and trance-like creative energy. In mythology, Neptune's ruler was the god of the seas and is linked to dreams. Since Neptune rules Pisces, the fish's sign that rules secret societies, sudden changes, and spiritual experiences, this placement is associated with the realms of the subconscious mind and higher consciousness. This is the downside of the placement because Neptune separates us from the physical world and absorbs us into the waters of our emotions.

Neptune in Pisces helps one connect to his inner emotions when he is also in tune with higher consciousness. This placement forces such an individual to find the spiritual energy within his soul that frees him from being obsessed with the material world; hence, Neptune's weakness is alienation. Some individuals may believe that they are special and free. Still, Neptune in the 12th house usually represents a secret or secret society that rules over the 12th house secrets; hence, these individuals may be tortured in their dreams or seek to explore realms of the psyche.

Pluto

Pluto is the last transpersonal planet, having been demoted following the discovery of Eris. Its power, however, has not diminished, and it rules Scorpio and the eighth house. In mythology, Pluto was the underworld god linked to power and transformation. It deals with death, transformation, secrets, sexuality, and wealth.

Pluto is a form of energy that has the power to transform us and give us the power we must evolve. Pluto rules matter and energy as it promotes the usual changes we experience in life due to time. Pluto's influence is disruptive because it forces us to face our hidden fears. Still, this placement reveals untapped resources we cannot use or are too afraid to utilize. These resources usually require intense and overwhelming emotional energy.

Healing Aspects

Healing aspects occur when two or more planetary bodies form an aspect of each other in the birth chart. These aspects create constructive energies that promote health, harmony, and abundance in your life. This healing enables a supportive connection between two or more planets that produces harmonious energy, and these planets are usually linked by friendship, love, or compassion.

The connections between the planets help minimize the negative energies produced when a planet's energy is projected onto other planets. However, when positive energies oppose negative energies, they cause these energies to cancel each other out, and the future is uncertain. These aspects are discussed further in the next chapter.

Chapter 6: Aspects in the Zodiac

Aspects are the angles formed by the planets and other celestial bodies in the horoscope. They weave together the disparate elements of the horoscope to form a cohesive story, and all aspects create a motivating element and some tension that inspires a person to act. There are other aspects, but the ones of focus here are conjunctions, oppositions, squares, and trines. These aspects reflect a basic confrontation between two forces or energies that either brings them together or pushes them apart. Each planet is associated with and symbolized by a certain energy. But these energies are not created equal. Some planets are simple, straightforward, and gentle; others have stronger energy and require more intense work to understand and work with. Some planets are more powerful in the horoscope than others and can profoundly affect a person's life.

A conjunction of two planets means that those two celestial bodies are sitting close together in the sky. This aspect of closeness can create a connection that cannot be ignored and that a person has to deal with. An opposition does the opposite - it forces two planets apart, and when this happens, the energy generated may feel like a falling out. Any aspect of the planets to another planet creates some interest or energy between the planets involved. A conjunction between Sun and Moon might represent a strong dependency between people and a need to care for one another. This relationship cannot grow without some effort toward compromise. When a planet is square another planet, it indicates a disagreement that creates tension. By itself, this aspect does not say anything about the nature of the disagreement, but by its nature, it is creating friction. Finally, a trine creates a harmonious relationship between the two planets, and this influence can help keep a person focused and on target.

. Jupiter represents wisdom and expansion, and as the planet of wisdom and expansion matures, it can greatly affect a person's life. A mature Jupiter brings great joy and well-being that can be very helpful in one's life. But a maturing Jupiter may begin to overstep its bounds and make its wisdom uncalled for or unwise, so

Planets are connected by aspects, which comprise an aspect of one planet to another, called a conjunction, and the relation of one planet to a planet in an adjacent house or opposition. Aspects are also composed of a degree from one planet to another planet. For example, if Moon is conjunct with Mars, Mars is 17°45′ strong when it is close to Moon. The degree of the planet, that is, its angular distance in degrees from the horizon to the Sun, is used to indicate the strength of aspects in a chart.

The aspect of planets and points to each other are called conjunctions, oppositions, and squares. Each aspect affects its own vertical house on the chart and every other vertical house associated with it. The closest aspect is known as the strongest aspect; the aspect furthest from the planet comes next in strength. The most important aspect of astrology is the Moon's conjunction with the Ascendant. Aspects are major points of interaction in a chart. The Sun conjuncts the Moon when these two bodies are most close together, forming a couple. The Moon conjuncts Mercury when these two bodies are closest together, which is a close relationship between two individuals. Mars is square Jupiter, which indicates a potential conflict between the two people. When Mars opposes Jupiter, this indicates a struggle between the two people.

Conjunction

A conjunction of two planets or bodies intensifies the symbolism of the planets and confuses the energies, making it difficult to separate and feel each planet's strengths. The conjunction may not be significant to Venus or Mercury, but that same conjunction may profoundly affect a person born with Uranus or Pluto prominent in their horoscope. The conjunction can also make it difficult to feel each planet's individuality. When there is a conjunction of two or more planets, a Numerology chart is often needed to delineate the planets' energies and assist in understanding their unique strengths.

A person's life is a story told in the stars, and the planets tell the story of life by weaving together the disparate elements into a cohesive whole. The elements are the planets and bodies in the horoscope. They influence each other and create the story of life, and weave the story together like a tapestry. Many people go through life looking for meaning in their experiences and trying to live more in accord with their true nature, but they are not always sure what "their true nature" is or why they may have struggled along. The planets help a person pick up the thread of the tapestry they are weaving. The planets help people connect to their deepest selves, making their lives more meaningful and fulfilling.

Opposition

The horoscope opposition is a discordant aspect, but the key to working with it is integrating the opposing energies. It is here where the most disharmony occurs between people. Suppose the opposition is between a Sun and a Chiron, for example. In that case, their energies are often at opposite ends of the spectrum, so one person may always be seeking comfort and never wanting to get out of their comfort zone; the other person might always be trying to get out there, experiencing as much of life as possible and always on the move. If these two people are in a relationship, the conflict will likely be very strong and long lasting.

The opposition aspect is the most discordant aspect of the zodiac, where one planet's representation must go against the energies of the other. The opposition aspect represents the struggle between needing to be needed and the desire for complete freedom. It is between needing to be accepted and feeling complete acceptance within oneself; it represents the conflict between needing to feel whole in contrast to feeling free.

When people are in a sensitive opposition, they may go through life feeling either like they have to be accepted by the other or the other way around. If they have difficulty understanding the conflict between them, they may feel as though they have to make up for the other person's judgment. The opposition between Mars and Pluto can represent the same struggle - between needing independence and needing intimacy, between needing to be aggressive and needing to be gentle and loving.

Trine

The trine aspect is the most harmonious aspect of the zodiac, and the planets complement and enrich each other effortlessly. A trine aspect is harmonious between two people when they get along well and have similar beliefs and values. This aspect represents feeling like a part of a pair. Many people experience harmony in a relationship when they have Venus opposite their Sun or Moon. A balanced trine aspect represents a relationship that is both a beautiful thing to be and a source of great joy to the person experiencing it.

The key to working with the trine aspect is freedom and flexibility. If one person is rigidly holding the relationship together, then the relationship is not likely to last. Both planets speak of harmony and balance, and each planet brings good things to the party. The individual represented by the Moon has sensitivity and emotional insight to help others through difficult times and difficulties. The individual represented by the Sun has vitality, energy, and stamina to keep the relationship going and keep it going for a long time. Both individuals are excellent at bringing confidence and inspiration to others, and both individuals are very positive and may bring inspired energy to a relationship. The trine aspect reveals our natural strengths, but because it flows so easily, we may not be aware of them. We can more easily fulfill our soul's potential when we begin to integrate our strengths into our daily lives.

Square

The square aspect represents the conflict between two planets or bodies. When there is a square between two planets, this indicates that one planet will always try to go against the other planet's energies. The square is the most difficult aspect to understand and work with because it represents what must be overcome or learned between people - and this tends to create conflict in a relationship.

When planets are square, they create disharmonious energy, which can feel ugly and difficult. In a square aspect, the planets are in the greatest tension with each other, yet they are affected by each other. This aspect provides the most impetus for the subject to break through evolutionary barriers. The key is to break through from one reality to another, to change one's point of view, and to learn something new. The key to working with this aspect is to choose to see the best in the other and to recognize that each person has something to offer the other that is valuable and important.

Semisquare

The semisquare is an exhale or night aspect that represents a barrier between two energies. It is easy to give up when things seem too difficult, but with patience and perseverance, you can move mountains. Sometimes we feel the most discouraged, but we only need to stand up and fight a little harder. The semisquare acts as a speed bump in our path - life's bumps that slow us down; it also acts as a gateway or a door that opens when we walk through it. The semisquare brings important information and asks us to pay attention. The semisquare is a bridge between the two planets yet does not fully express the energy of either one of them.

Sesquisquare

The sesquisquare aspect reflects the challenge and tension of the opposing forces. The sesquisquare aspect is between a square and an opposition, so the energies between the two planets are intensified by the energies between the two signs.

Quintile

A quintile is a day aspect that creates a 72° angle in the chart between two planets. This characteristic typically denotes creative ability, particularly about patterns and structures. The natal chart typically indicates an artistic talent, particularly in terms of artistic ability in the worlds of painting, sculpture, architecture, music, dance, or drama. From a practical viewpoint, it often suggests a talent for creative carpentry, woodworking, or other creative do-it-yourself activities. There may be a tendency to collect things of interest. The natal chart with a quintile typically suggests a talent for creative decoration.

This aspect also typically suggests a talent for construction or decorative arts.

Semisextile

Because the signs are different modalities and elements, the semisextile aspect is difficult to interpret. Still, some believe that the zodiac is ordered this way on purpose and that each sign builds on the one before it.

Sextile

The sextile aspect connects two planets that are roughly 60 degrees apart. It is a harmonious aspect that opens up pathways to growth with enormous potential. In a trine aspect, the energy of the planets is almost in sync - they complement each other and harmonize so well that the planets are in complete harmony. In a sextile aspect, the two planets are not in harmony but balanced by each other: the energies of both planets add to the energies of the other and form a balanced and harmonious blend.

For example, if Venus is a person's ruling planet, the energy of Venus square Saturn may create an obstacle to a person's ego that moves us away from what feels safe and comfortable. On the other hand, the energy of the opposition creates an opportunity for a person with a square Venus to expand their consciousness and awareness, which can result in personal growth and inner awakening.

Inconjunct

The inconjunct is a difficult aspect that involves planets in various elements and modalities; you cannot combine the two, and you must accept the necessity of compartmentalization. The planets are not in harmony and are not balanced, but each planet affects the other on the planet's level.

A person whose Venus is quincunx or inconjunct Saturn in Capricorn will be torn between the desire to play and the desire to work hard and build great security. This person may find it difficult to choose either one or the other because both feel equally desirable and ennobling. Another person with Venus quincunx Saturn may make different choices - working hard to build security or playing hard, spending all they have, gambling, or working long hours. Hence, they never have any security or money.

It is difficult for the planets to be in this position together because they resist each other. The planets are in a dangerous position but will not destroy each other because they are not in harmony. The planets are out of balance with each other - one planet is too strong and the other is too weak –- the effect of this is that the planet that is in discord is out of harmony with the rest of the forces working in the world, as a result of the conjunction or opposition.

Harmonic Charts

Harmonic charts seek to unite planets in a chart that works together. Each harmonic chart rearranges aspects connected by the number of that harmony chart, making the aspect connections more visible.

Highly Aspected Planets

The planet with the most aspects from other planets and essential bodies is an important part of any interpretation. This planet reflects the matter at hand. For example, a person whose

Moon is in Cancer might be concerned with issues including mother, family, security, or the home.

Essential Bodies

Essential bodies are those bodies that move very little. The Moon rules over essential bodies such as the tides of the oceans. The Sun rules over celestial bodies because it warms our land and atmosphere. Because the planets can trine and square essential bodies, even though they do not directly touch them, these planets can influence the planets that touch them. Because there is so much information to integrate, the most aspected planet is a strong focal point for the astrological sign, but it can also lead to hyper analysis.

Chapter 7: The Astrological Houses

The planets and other essential bodies, signs, and houses comprise the horoscope, representing your soul's evolutionary potential in this lifetime. Your birth horoscope is a map of your soul's evolutionary trajectory. The map reflects the order of life's stages that unfold according to universal laws. It's here to help you understand that your present condition is the outcome of your personal choices, but you can choose to move in a good direction by consciously creating your life.

Your birth chart signifies your soul's evolution potential in your current lifetime. The actions you take and the choices you make determine how you actualize that potential. This continual co-creation is the essence of free will: the Golden Key to discovering your True Self. Thus, your birth chart becomes the map that can guide you forward in life.

Your birth chart reflects many influences, including your karma, birthdate, and the positions of the planets and the Sun, all of which are based on your exact time of birth. Your birth chart delineates the soul's evolutionary potential in seven essential areas of life: soul evolution, soul purpose, soul relationships, soul missions, soul destiny, spiritual opportunities, and soul potential.

Your birth chart is as unique as your fingerprint. Some elements will always be the same; others will vary according to location. The 12 houses represent areas of life or fields of experience, as well as a pulse or breath of the cosmos, with the first house representing a day house or inhale and the second house representing a night house or exhale. These houses are measured along the horizon, extending from east to west. At birth, the Sun is placed in one of the houses. When the Sun moves into another house, the moveable zodiac wheel is aligned accordingly, called "ascension."

Here is an overview of the different astrological houses and how they can affect your personality and outlook in your birth chart.

First House

The first house is associated with birth and childhood. It's a day, action-oriented, angular house, and the sign represents the eastern horizon at the time and place of birth in the horoscope, as seen from that time and place's perspective. This sign's influence denotes your personality and outlook during the daytime hours. The first house also represents the physical body. Its element is Fire, and its quality is cardinal. As a terrestrial house, it represents the family. Its ruler is Mars.

The self is most sharply focused in this house's sphere of influence. Recovery from loss occurs through direct experience and action.

Second House

The second house represents possessions, the accumulated value of lifetime experiences, income, and asset investment. The sign on the cusp indicates the house of money in the horoscope. This sign's influence denotes your outlook and personality during the nighttime hours.

Also associated with finances, such as budgets, taxes, investments, and returns, the second house is ruled by Venus, governing desires. Its element is Earth, and its quality is mutable. It is a nocturnal house representing your birth family and home. This house influences your dwell in the realm of the material or physical. This is the moment of fulfillment in the physical world.

Third House

The third house indicates communication, conversation, and the mind. It also shows where loved ones reside and travel. This house represents friends and affiliations.

We learn to observe the world around us, find our voice, learn to write, and develop our communication styles in the third house. It's associated with the family, including parental influences and home life. The third house's ruler is Mercury.. This influences your ability to change and grow.

Fourth House

The fourth house is the foundation of our emotional and material security. It is the stage at which we become aware of our inner emotional landscape and how we emotionally respond to the world around us. It reflects our foundations and associations, including the people we live with or spend time with and how our family life influences us.

The fourth house is night-oriented. It is associated with the family and life's unconscious or "dark" side. This house is associated with nostalgia and fortune through the various legacies of life. It rules heritage and tradition. Its sign in the zodiac is Cancer, representing the house of community or siblings in the horoscope. Its quality is feminine, and its ruler is the Moon.

Fifth House

The fifth house is all about our social interactions and physical activities. Through the five senses, we become aware of our physical environment and experience the world through our senses. Children are represented in this house. A planet's quadrant of effect is also felt in the fifth house.

This house represents a nocturnal environment and is ruled by the Sun. It can activate or create action, affecting us socially or physically. This house covers partnerships and has a masculine quality.

Sixth House

The sixth house is associated with the earth sign Virgo, and Mercury rules it. It represents our daily activities and jobs. This house corresponds to innate skills, talents, and subconscious tendencies one cannot control. The house ruler is associated with the mind and intellect.

With a background in the physical sciences, the sixth house is traditionally associated with the work world. It is associated with your connection with your physical surroundings and subconscious tendencies.

Seventh House

The seventh house correlates to the area of romantic relationships. The sign on the cusp represents the house of partnership in the birth chart. Its ruler is Venus, and its ruling emotion is love. Its element is air and has a mutable quality. It also represents friendships, communication exchanges or written communication, and contracts.

It also correlates to marriage and divorce, intimacy and love.It rules the sex act and fertility in the horoscope. Its sign represents the house of elderly care or elderly dependents in the horoscope, and its quality is masculine.

Eighth House

The eighth house is the realm of secrets, what lies beyond our physical world and our comprehension. This house governs secrets in the zodiac. Its ruler is Pluto, and its quality is feminine as it correlates to deep-seated emotions and hard work.

This house in the birth chart represents the house of retirement or elderly care. The eighth house signifies psychological death and regeneration, a new beginning, and writing the obituary for this model of the world you've known - releasing what is no longer useful to you to embrace the new and unknown, which will be an integral part of your future.

Ninth House

This house represents mental and spiritual or philosophical pursuits, communication, and long-distance travel. Courts and rulers occupy this house. Higher knowledge is governed in this house, ruled by the planet of intuition, Jupiter.

This house is the realm of the distant past and can indicate foreign roots or origins. The sign on the cusp signifies the house of groups or siblings in the natal chart. Its sign is Sagittarius. Higher education and personal beliefs are all associated with the ninth house. It is a house representing a quest for meaning in life.

Tenth House

The tenth house represents your public reputation or status and is the most visible part of your horoscope. It is a gravitas place where you can build financial and physical security, and Saturn and Capricorn rule it. Its cusp sign in the horoscope and signifies changing jobs frequently for your career or moving from place to place.

It is the house of wealth accrual and investors or investment bankers. It rules partnerships, business relationships, large institutions, and large and important undertakings - the structures necessary to support us in a materialistic world. It is associated with generational change and may be full of promise for abundance and attainment.

Eleventh House

The eleventh house is related to social causes, social consciousness, politics, and groups of friends, organizations, and associations. It denotes resources and influences through friendships and associates. As a Uranus-ruled sign, it represents the house of leisure, social actions, groups, or groups in marriage in the horoscope.

It is the realm of philosophical ideas and organizations or groups and reflects the conscious and subconscious desire because we are social beings. It correlates to the humanitarian side of life.

Twelfth House

This house represents altered states, the prenatal experience, and the period of fading before the final exhalation. It connects us to transpersonal understanding and knowledge.

It is a lonely place ruled by the planet of hidden secrets, Neptune. It indicates challenges on the physical or spiritual plane or thoughts of death and transformation. It rules werewolves, vampires, the necromantic side of life, and mortality. It also correlates to the time of death in mythology because it is the house of dissolution. It represents the end of your world if you have chosen to let go of it.

Understanding the astrological houses in your birth chart ensures that you seek and discover their meaning within you and apply them to your destiny rather than to a meaningless chart with no emotional attachment. Learning each astrological house's meaning makes your perception of yourself much more peaceful, explored, and knowledgeable. Alongside your interpretation and application, you can learn to harness the power of astrological houses and understand why they influence your destiny. When you are available to them and embrace them consciously, you can use them to your advantage to achieve your highest and best good and to help others. Astrology allows you to become aware of and accept your true potential and highest calling.

Chapter 8: Understanding your Birth Chart

This chapter will go over the astrological elements of signs, houses, and planets and how they play a role in the formation of the birth chart. Rather than focusing on the function of the planet or house in question, or the meaning of its sign position, the focus will be on the mythology behind each astrology sign and the generalizations we make about the people who fall under it. This will better explain why we perceive certain planets and signs in certain houses as "good" or "bad" omens.

The twelve zodiac signs are the constellations that cross the sky in the ecliptic during the year of birth. In the Western tradition, the zodiac starts at the winter solstice (December 21st) and extends through the remainder of the arc, ending at the summer solstice (June 21st). A planet or house sign will represent the qualities associated with its constellation or house.

The outer rim of an astrological horoscope represents the zodiac, and the belt represents the 12 astrological signs. The 12 signs represent the different psychological impulses and needs. Symbols in the signs and houses represent the planets and other essential bodies, and each planet shows a different aspect of the psyche.

This chapter will expand on what you have already learned and introduce some new aspects of horoscope interpretation. We will discuss the archetypes and mythological stories behind the constellations, the signs, and the planets. From here, you will learn how the planets affect us from an astrological perspective and why we think that certain planets and signs become helpful in guiding our lives.

The astrological houses help to organize a chart and reveal important information about a person's personality, behavior, and character. The aspects between planets or points within a chart reveal important details regarding a particular encounter or partnership. An astrological chart or horoscope is a symbolic representation of the positions of the planets and other astrological objects on the Earth at the time of an event, such as birth. The placement of the planets and other objects on an astrological chart and their astrological alignments are used to predict future events in a person's life.

The sign position of the planets and houses further define the individual's life circumstances, but to interpret this symbolism, we must first understand the astrological symbolism behind the zodiac signs. Let's begin our astrological journey through the zodiac with the constellations. The constellations form a part of the earth's field of energy in motion, and just as astrologers read the sun signs, they also read the zodiac signs. Each constellation represents a different aspect of a person's psyche and a different part of consciousness. Much like humans have genetically inherited a set of predispositions, so does the planets' constellation read in the birth chart. The planets in the natal chart represent a psychological blueprint that each of us possesses from birth.

In a natal chart, the planet's position affects health and well-being and represents the individual's psychological makeup. The synchronicity between the planets in the birth chart and the planets in each individual's constellation, or sign, defines the landscape of a person's personality and characteristics. In other words, the constellations help define the person's general temperament and life circumstances.

The Big Three

The three primary personality indicators are the Sun, Moon, and Ascendant. According to the astrologer's perspective, the personality and appearance of a person are a direct result of the angles formed between the Sun and the Moon in a birth chart. Their relationship forms the basis for both physical and psychological disposition.

Sun

The luminary, or Sun, represents an individual's sense of identity, confidence, warmth, willpower, and leadership ability. This celestial body governs your integration into society, objectivity, communication ability, life force, vitality, and growth. The luminaries are indicators of self-esteem and self-worth. The Sun symbolizes our basic identity and emotional reality.

The Sun is your orchestra's conductor and represents your ego, vital self, and the present. This is the main zodiac sign you select in your horoscope because your ego is the center of your personality. The Sun is the center of your solar system and represents your self-concept. It tells you about your existence and how you view the world. It defines your attitude toward life and how you express your sense of logic, nature, and personality.

The Moon

The Moon represents emotion, sensitivity, intuition, receptivity, feelings, and intuition. The conjunction of the Moon with the Sun indicates a person oriented to the outside world and extroverted nature. The proximity of the Moon to the Sun indicates awareness and emotional capacity. The Earth's orbit creates the polarity of the Sun and Moon and produces lunar phases. These phases apply to astrology as well. The new Moon stage represents the beginning of a new cycle, and the creation of the new cycle involves the configuration of the Sun and Moon in a certain way. A full Moon represents a climax or culmination in the cycle and describes the middle position of the Moon in the cycle. The last quarter stage represents the end of a cycle, or the completion of the current suit of cards in the deck, and this occurs when the phase of the Moon is waning.

The Moon represents feelings largely dependent on the sign in which it is placed. The Moon represents your emotional energy, so knowing the sign in which your Moon falls will help you analyze how your emotional self has developed or has developed in certain ways.

Eclipses

In astrology, solar and lunar eclipses indicate imbalances in the Sun and Moon's relationship. During an eclipse period, the luminaries are shadowed by Earth, and the Moon entirely or partially leaves the Earth's shadow for a period of days and months. The Moon returns to its regular orbit around the Earth and back into its shadow, where it casts its shadow on the Earth. This shadow period is a time of reflection. An eclipse further indicates an increasing dissonance between an individual's sense of self and reality, as represented in the eclipse. The shadow period is a time to evaluate how one perceives the world and what is true about it and those residing there. During this phase, one drifts into the mind oneself in the process of self-reflection. It is a period when belief systems are tested, values are questioned, and the self is examined. It is a time to look at one's inner world, represented by the Sun and Moon in their birth chart.

The Four Parts on your Birth Chart

Ascendant

The ascendant is the sign and degree on the eastern horizon at the time and location of birth or the beginning of any event. It represents the aspect of yourself that you show the rest of the world. The Ascendant represents your self-image and how others perceive you. It represents your public image and personality, how you introduce yourself to others, and how you show yourself to the world.

Your rising sign can also indicate your early childhood home environment. It becomes the wall you may show others when you are in an unfamiliar situation or with new acquaintances. An ascendant that rises in the same degree of two different signs represents two sides of your personality.

Descendant

The descendant aspect in your natal chart is your lowered angle or the fall of the planets. The descendant sign symbolizes your subconscious self and how you are feeling on the inside. You generally fail to share the hidden aspect of your personality with others. .

Midheaven

The Medium Coeli, or Midheaven in your birth chart, is your star chart's highest point. It is at the peak of your ascension and signifies your social status, personal value, and involvement in the world, represented by the tenth house in your natal chart. It describes how you receive and express your power in the world. The Midheaven represents your position in life, leadership qualities, and ambition. Aspects between the Sun and Midheaven describe your social image, expression of power, and image of yourself.

Nadir

The Imum Coeli or Nadir in your natal chart indicates your chart's lowest point. It is where the planets are making a big dip downward or close to the point of their lowest orbit. This celestial body represents your hidden self and influences your subconscious nature, personal causes and motivations, personal insecurity, and feeling victimized. The sign of the Nadir describes any level of discomfort you may have with parts of the self that should be treated more objectively.

Your Ruling Planet

Your Ascendant's ruling planet is recognized to be your ruling planet. Therefore, the planet at the top of your chart represents what you are trying to achieve and how you try to build your success. Of course, since your Sun faces outward and is in a position in your chart that everyone shares, it more personifies your hopes and wishes. For example, if a person has Pisces on their Ascendant sign and Neptune rules their eleventh house, it means that this person is most likely to be secretly afraid of their panic attacks, and their greatest desire is to feel safe and nurtured.

On the other hand, the person has Mars in the sixth house ruled by Mercury, which means that this person has an innate sexual drive, but doesn't necessarily know how to express that. This person wants to find the perfect partner with whom they can make love to their heart's desire. This person's greatest fear is being rejected or abandoned. However, this person has great power to overcome his fears.

Stellium

A stellium is three or more planets in the same sign. A stellium in your birth chart related to a ruling planet is important, as it indicates an intensely strong emphasis on the sign with the sign and house that the planet rules. These planets indicate a dominant, highly functional part of your personality that pushes itself forward in life. The more planets are involved, the more powerful the energy aspect is.

Mutually-Receptive Planets

When two planets are in mutual reception, they support each other, but each planet's strength determines the strength of that support. A planet is less strong when in the same sign as another planet. The existence of mutual reception indicates that these planets help each other, but it tends to produce unexpected results. If the planets make a harmonious aspect, their strengths combine positively. However, if the planets make discordant aspects, their energies do not combine well, and their combined energies are unharmonious.

Chiron and non-Planetary Celestial Objects

Chiron is an astrologically unique body because he has human front legs, a human head, and a torso. In Greek Mythos, he was a teacher, healer, and archer. He is referred to as the wounded healer, the rainbow bridge between spirit and matter, and the maverick shaman. Chiron's symbol, shaped like a key, indicates some type of connecting or unlocking energy. It may be the lock that opens a doorway or a key that protects against spiritual invasion.

Astrologically, Chiron is known as an asteroid. It is often referred to as "The Centaur" or "The Universal Teacher", indicating its inter-relationships with nature and spirit. It takes a person away from human limits and into a greater spiritual connection with nature and the universe. Chiron is associated with the planet Neptune. It follows another asteroid's path and appears to move between those two bodies.

In astrology, Chiron is believed to influence our healing abilities, intuitions, psychic and spiritual abilities, and creative skills. He is also the gateway between the zodiac's sensitive and defensive signs and the zodiac's fixed signs. Being born with a Chiron stellium shows that you are destined to be a healer in some capacity. This is likely a field you will gravitate towards, and you will find fulfillment in this line of work.

When Chiron turns retrograde, it activates a very difficult period. You may experience a sort of breakdown, or it may be that you reach a life-changing decision that catapults you into a new direction. Chiron retrograde can be hard work, but you have the internal resources to weather periods like this.

Vesta

Vesta, the goddess of the signs Virgo and Scorpio, represents the eternal flame that burns within each of us. She represents the Vestal Virgins, specifically chosen because they were not yet deflowered. These women were devoted to Vesta and made sacrifices for her to keep the flame alive. When Vesta moves near the Sun, the planet begins to burn hotter, and when Vesta travels near Saturn, the planet becomes colder.

Vesta signifies commitment and focus. She represents our innermost passion or wishes that is ignited when faced with strong opposition from others or when trying to achieve a goal we willed ourselves to achieve. She represents unconditional love and the intense commitment we can potentially show to others.

Being born under one of these signs indicates that Vesta has significance in your life. Vesta theories suggest that when Vesta appears near the Sun, it indicates that there will be a period of increased stability. When Vesta appears near Saturn, it may indicate that there will be a time of great sorrow.

Ceres

Ceres, the Great Mother, is associated with the signs Cancer, Virgo, and Taurus, and she represents how we nurture and meet our own needs. She is associated with material abundance, so having the planet in Taurus indicates that you have a deep need for the material world. You are likely to hold onto things longer than others. For a person born with the sign of Cancer, there is a need for security and routine. You may be possessive and overly attached to family, friends, or interests, but your nurturing and generosity are also excellent traits.

The element of Earth rules Ceres, and she deals with issues like material resources and how money is handled. Because of her placement in Taurus, she is about growth and harvest. She tends to transform resources into riches. Ceres can also indicate the natural birth cycle, pregnancy, or motherhood. She represents the fertility of the Earth and how we nurture it.

When achieving personal goals and assisting others in taking responsibility for themselves, a person with Ceres in Capricorn in the first house feels heightened self-worth. They feel secure in their role as a parent and feel that their personal needs are balanced with time spent as a family and supporting family members.

Pallas Athena

Pallas Athena is a warrior goddess and the goddess of wisdom. She is associated with the ability to make sense of complex patterns and the soul's desire to move beyond the binary world, and she rules the signs of Libra, Leo, and Aquarius. This goddess represents intelligence, intellect, strategy, and strategic thinking skills in astrology. In your birth chart, she represents the understanding of complicated patterns and visions. Pallas is symbolic when separating yourself from others' viewpoints. She is efficient and gets straight to the point. She allows you to see where you need to make changes and how to see all possible solutions.

Juno

Juno, the asteroid, represents meaningful relationships and the oppressed and is associated with Libra and Scorpio signs. She rules over marriage and children. When Juno appears near a planet in your birth chart, it suggests a time of great bonding, the development of a closer relationship, or a time that will be better for you financially. If a planet receives support from Juno, it suggests that things will go smoothly. However, if the planet conflicts with Juno, there may be problems. A person with a Juno stellium may enjoy a deep and lasting marriage.

Juno's element is Fire. She brings a lot of passion into the equation regarding relationships and marital stability. She motivates you to go after your goals and desires for a relationship. She shows your motivation in finding someone special to share your life with.

When entering into a long-term partnership or marriage, a Juno in Libra in the first house indicates feelings of self-doubt and an inability to trust yourself. You may need to sacrifice personal goals to commit more fully to your partner. This is a good thing in the long run because your partnership can benefit both of you in other capacities outside your married state, such as raising children or finding success at a career level.

Chapter 9: Your Birth Chart Interpretation

The finer points of birth chart interpretation will be covered in this chapter, including hemisphere emphasis, the Moon's nodes, the Part of Fortune, retrograde planets, intercepted signs, and transits. We will explain how these indicators work in tandem to provide a more comprehensive explanation of the natal chart.

Nodes

Nodes in your birth chart are the north and south lunar nodes, which mark the elongation of the lunar orbit on the ecliptic. They are like repetitious gravity points in the Earth's orbit, where the position of the Moon and other planets shift. These points are referred to as "nodes" because, in ancient college texts, they were mistaken for the horns of the Moon.

North Node

The North Node is the area of the Moon's path that moves through the constellations of the north part of the sky: first Aquarius, then Pisces, and finally Aries. The Moon moves through the constellations roughly every twenty-nine days; hence, in one lunar year, or roughly 354 days, the Moon will jump to a different sky area.

The North Node corresponds to the area of life in which you find your eventual fulfillment. This area of life is signified by the Moon's location on the ecliptic as viewed from Earth, and your destiny in this life will depend on how effectively you have achieved your goals in this area. The North Node is like the center of a clock: when the Moon moves to its natal position, it is most directly opposite the west point of Earth's axis. In contrast, the South Node is opposite the eastern point of the Earth's axis.

In the birth chart, where the natal planets are denoted by the zodiacal degrees in which they lie, the north node is usually the furthest point away from the planet. This way, it is connected to the planets more closely than the south node. It may lie in the eighth house in traditional astrology, but this is not the only place it may occur. Any sign may have a North Node, and any planet may have a North Node within an aspected sign.

The following is a summary of the meaning of the North Nodes:

First House: Foster independence, bravery, spontaneity, and self-awareness.

Second House: Develop strong values, self-worth, a connection with the Earth and the senses, patience, and loyalty.

Third House: Develop your curiosity, listening skills, openness to new ideas and perspectives, and tact.

Fourth House: Develop empathy, the ability to notice and validate feelings, humility, and awareness and acceptance of the feelings and moods of others.

Fifth House: Develop self-confidence, creative self-expression, a willingness to stand out, and a sense of playfulness and fun.

Sixth House: Develop a sense of service, pay more attention to routines and details, exercise moderation, and take compassionate action.

Seventh House: Improve your ability to collaborate, diplomacy, awareness of others' needs, how to live and work with others, and sharing.

Eighth House: Learn to be less attached to material worth, to be aware of others' psychological desires and motives, and to share power dynamics.

Ninth House: Develop an awareness of and trust in your intuition or guidance from the source, a sense of adventure and self-confidence, and an awareness of higher consciousness.

Tenth House: Develop self-control and respect, as well as maturity in situations, responsibility, and self-reliance.

Eleventh House: Develop self-approval and a willingness to share inventive and unconventional ideas, work in groups and connect with humanity in an egalitarian and humanitarian way, and connect with people who share your interests.

Twelfth House: Develop compassion, trust in and surrender to the source or the principle of collective creation, unconditional love, a spiritual path, and self-reflective practices.

Since the North Node represents the area of life in which you will find fulfillment, you will also find a creative iffiness of visualization in this area of life. The North Node also rules self-assertion, so you will often be less concerned about what other people think if you pursue the goals this Node represents.

South Node

The South Node is the cosmos area associated with the signs of the southern part of the sky: first Scorpio, then Sagittarius, and finally Capricorn. It corresponds roughly to the farthest point of the Moon's path from Earth. The South Node resembles the

North Node in that the natal planets in the birth chart are furthest away from this lunar point. Any sign may have a South Node, and any planet may have a South Node within an aspected sign. The general trend of planets in the natal chart should go from the closest point to the farthest point.

Here are some details of the south nodes in different houses:

First House: Work to loosen the grip of impulsiveness, unhealthy selfishness, anger issues, and over-assertiveness in the first house.

Second House: Work to lessen stubborn tendencies, resistance to change, over-attachment to ownership and accumulation of material possessions, overeating, and other overindulgences.

Third House: Work to reduce the impact of indecision, the belief that you always need more information or study before acting, ignoring intuition, and trusting other people's opinions and ideas over your own.

Fourth House: Work to reduce reliance on others, insecurity, emotional manipulation, risk avoidance, and over-attachment to fears and safety.

Fifth House: Work to reduce your need for others' approval and admiration, as well as your sense of entitlement, risk-taking, and melodramatic tendencies.

Sixth House: Work to reduce tendencies to over-give to the point of self-sacrifice, difficulties receiving from others, analysis paralysis, anxiety and worry, and over-criticism.

Seventh House: Work to reduce selflessness, playing nice to the detriment of yourself and others, codependence, and only seeing yourself through the eyes of others.

Eighth House: Work to reduce obsessive or compulsive habits, preoccupation with others' motivations and actions, hyper-reactivity and irritation with others, and attraction to crises.

Ninth House: Work to lessen your tendency to be dogmatic and self-righteous, to not listen to what others are saying, to talk over others, and to speak before thinking things through.

Tenth House: Work to reduce the need to be in control of and responsible for everything and everyone, appear strong at all times and be overly goal-oriented.

Eleventh House: Work to refrain from your tendency to withdraw from emotional situations and appear cold, to avoid confrontation, and to shapeshift to fit in with the crowd. Hence, you feel accepted rather than embracing your uniqueness.

Twelfth House: Work to reduce oversensitivity and victimization, withdrawal and easy giving up, extreme escapism and avoidance of the "real" world, and self-doubt.

Since the South Node corresponds to the area of life where you need to accomplish your destiny, it represents the area of your life where you have untapped potential. It also rules the development of your underlying motives and fears of inadequacy. The South Node represents your fears and illusions of inadequacy, which can stand in the way of your full development.

Lunar Nodes

The lunar nodes are the points on the Moon's orbit where it intersects the ecliptic. The lunar nodes refer to signs opposite each other on the ecliptic: the north lunar node is opposite the region of Pisces, while the south lunar node is in the opposite region of Virgo. If you are born at night, the Moon and any planets near the lunar nodes will be visible, lying at the outermost part of the visible hemisphere.

The Moon's nodes represent the soul's past and future and are a developmental continuum. While the North Node correlates with your sense of individuality and uniqueness, the South Node correlates with your sense of permanent identity. The South Node has more to do with destiny than the North Node, which deals with more immediate needs: it deals with goals that are broader and more important than your immediate needs.

Because the lunar node cycle lasts about 18.5 years, people born 9 years before or after us are our nodal opposites. The ancients believed that these nodal periods, or life cycles, are the window of time in our lives when we are most open to change and transformation.

Another aspect of the lunar nodes is their relation to the nodes of planets in the birth chart. The nodes of the moon are called the lunar nodes. The moon's North Node is associated with the first, sixth, and ninth house points. The moon's South Node is associated with the fifth, seventh, and tenth house points.

Part of Fortune

The Part of Fortune is the area of your birth chart where the Sun is positioned when the Moon is furthest from Earth. It, therefore, takes the place of the North Node in a person's chart when the natal moon is closest to the Sun and in Capricorn. This rules the areas of life you seek out rather than being sought out by others; these areas of life reflect areas of potential fulfillment. The Part of Fortune is like the place where a potentially successful person lives: they can practice their talents without outside interference. It is a self-sufficient area and is ruled by Jupiter. For example, if born on October 21, it is the sign Libra, ruled by

Venus. When Venus is dignified and in Libra, people can transform their talents into success. This area of life is difficult when Venus is debilitated or out of dignity. Venus is never afflicted in Libra, indicating Hera's gift to women.

The Part of Fortune expresses how you naturally relate with others. If the Part of Fortune is in Capricorn, you will be an outgoing person in your birth chart. You feel comfortable around other people and can comfortably share your ideas without discomfort. Libra is a sign that rules relationships with others, so the person with a Part of Fortune in Libra tends to be sociable. If a person has a Part of Fortune in Cancer, that person will be more introverted and reserved.

The Part of Fortune indicates where you might find fortune and abundance, and the sign and house hint where you might find it. For example, if born in the sign of Libra on October 21, the Part of Fortune would be in the tenth house.

The Part of Fortune is a subsection of the Ascendant. The three parts of the Part of Fortune are the daytime planet Venus, the nighttime planet Jupiter, and the Midheaven sector. The Part of Fortune shines a light on the areas of life that define the individual. Planets in retrograde motion are planets that appear to be moving backward in the sky from our vantage point on Earth. Planets in this configuration are "stationing" and taking the time to reflect on themselves or what is happening around them. Planets in reverse motion often inspire feelings of order and predictability. Retrograde planets often indicate a need for introspection and reflection.

Retrogrades

When a planet moves retrograde, it turns backward in the sky. Because a planet's position supplies archetypal meanings, the retrograde planet becomes an "old god," "old witch," or "old demon" as it turns backward above its natal position. Retrograde planets often invoke repressed feelings of loss, discouragement, lack of support, and so forth. Retrograde planets show their influence most intensely during the two weeks before and two weeks after they turn retrograde.

During a planet's retrograde period, you may often experience feelings that contradict your conscious desires. Retrograde planets put you in touch with feelings associated with the planet in your birth chart that you have not yet dealt with. If the planet is in direct motion and you are mentally and emotionally mature enough, you can use this effect to push yourself forward in areas of life that you need to face. For example, if Saturn were retrograde, it would indicate the areas that you need to slow down and reflect more before moving ahead. Saturn retrograde could challenge you to look back at your mistakes and give a better idea of what you need to know before taking the risk.

Retrograde planets often indicate a clear turning point in the evolution of a person's life, and planets in this motion give you a chance to examine your life and examine your attitudes, habits, and patterns of behavior. It is important to pay attention to what the planet is indicating and then act upon your decisions. Use your intuition regularly to develop and learn interesting and useful things.

When a planet appears to move backward from our perspective on Earth, it is said to be retrograde. The retrograde impacts the planet's appearance to retrace a zodiac area from our perspective, making its energy more palpable. Because the planet appears to move backward in the sky, it resonates with the past rather than the present and may affect dreams connected to the past, including nightmares. This energy is associated with obsession, obsession leads to compulsion, and the compulsion can lead to depression, despair, and confusion.

If retrograde planets appear in a natal chart, the person may feel out of place in that society or alien to the dominant culture. For example, when Jupiter turns retrograde in the sign of Virgo, we will have a radically different attitude about authority than we normally do. Because Jupiter rules our sense of self-worth and relatedness to others, we may feel less worthy or even downright ugly.

The most common retrograde we experience is Mercury since this planet has the shortest orbit around the sun. When this planet appears to move backward in the galaxy, it differs from a normal Mercury transit in that it lasts longer and affects the entire group. For example, when Mercury turns retrograde, it will turn retrograde for about 4 to 6 weeks in one area of the zodiac and return to its original location on the other side of the zodiac, stopping at several other points along the way. During this period, you will feel the effects of the planet much more strongly than with a simple Mercury transit. Retrograde Mercury disrupts communication and causes delays in academic endeavors when learning new information, causing the information to become messy.

During Mercury retrograde, mistakes in speech and communication are common, and the messy flow of communication can result in chaos. However, it is common to have important breakthroughs during this time, and this energy brings fertile ground where you can initiate new relationships. Mercury retrograde is a period of both release and transformation.

The Hemispheres

The astrological chart's eastern hemisphere emphasizes day, inhale energy, and describes self-determined, goal-oriented, and intentional people. In the astrological birth chart, the eastern hemisphere is opposite the western hemisphere, which emphasizes the planets disappearance to the west during the night and appearance in the east come morning.

In a birth chart's western hemisphere, the Sun expresses the self's compulsion for growth and expansion and the outer edges of Selfhood. The Moon in the opposite hemisphere is associated with an intuitive grasp of the mental realm of consciousness, the inner feelings of emotion, and the secret desires of identity. In the western hemisphere, these people are more likely to succumb to peer pressure at night. Their identity is ruled by desire and instinct.

Eclipses

When the Earth's shadow falls on the Moon, a lunar eclipse occurs, and a solar eclipse occurs when the Moon blocks the Sun. In astrology, eclipses are feared because they take away the focus of light. Because eclipses last approximately 3 hours, the time when the eclipse is at its peak is the time of maximum disruption and instability.

Eclipses are related to Spades, Swords, and Cups in the Minor Arcana of the Tarot. A solar eclipse is related to Death and Temperance, an eclipse of the Moon is related to the Queen of Spades, and an eclipse of the Sun is related to The Chariot. A lunar eclipse is related to The Moon, and The Tower, an eclipse of Mercury is related to The Knight of Cups, and an eclipse of Venus is related to The King of Swords.

Eclipses can be a time of chaos in people's lives. They are often a time of change that can lead toward greater abundance and prosperity. If such an event occurs in your life, be prepared for the unexpected. Look to Virgo and Capricorn for an attitude of objectivity and balance.

Astrologically, Moon eclipses are considered more powerful because the Moon represents our emotions. Saturn's retrograde period can act as a time of self-analysis or reflection. When Mercury turns retrograde, you may find yourself bumping into people and re-visiting situations from your past. Neptune's influence during Neptune's retrograde could indicate a need for more reflection and consideration before acting. The good aspect of a retrograde is that it reveals hidden areas of life that you must explore more completely. If you pay attention to your dreams, you will know when Pluto's retrograde period starts and ends because your dreams will be much more intense and life will be much more emotionally charged.

When using unequal house systems, such as those of Placidus, Porphyry, or Koch, intercepted signs occur. These house systems operate on a time basis, and opposing houses are always the same size. When intercepting a sign in the natal chart, the person must consciously learn to access that sign's energy. People with an intercepted sign often experience what they have blocked out in childhood. People born in the sign of Scorpio often have deep and painful experiences.

People born under a negative planet or sign may have a tragic experience. When the sign of Libra is intercepted in a birth chart, it may be a negative time in that person's life because Libra is the sign of relationships and balance. Libra's negative polarity is the sign of Scorpio, which Mars rules. When Scorpio intercepts Libra in a birth chart, the person may experience Scorpio's trigon of seduction, which is all about sexual energy.

The hemisphere of your birth chart defines your habitual emotional and behavioral attitudes. You might find it easy to explain your behavior because you recognize yourself in words that describe your personality.

Transits

Transits are a method of forecasting trends and personal development by combining the transiting planet's keywords by sign and house. In astrology, a planetary transit can affect you by temporarily disrupting or speeding up your life, depending on whether you are naturally predisposed to such a speed and stream of events. Your natal chart indicates your predisposition for growth and provides insight into what you do best.

Because Neptune and Pluto have long cycles, planetary returns are one of the most important ways to examine transits. Knowledge of the power of manifestation can improve your life. There are many techniques, such as setting goals, visualizing, affirmations, meditation, and using numerology and astrology to develop abundance and prosperity in your life.

Astrologically, long-term cycles repeat over and over again through the centuries. These patterns are called nodal cycles about the two lunar nodes. The nodes are the points where the moon's orbit crosses the ecliptic plane or the sun's path through the sky. There is a one-year cycle involving the two nodes, and they switch positions in the zodiac every 19 years. The cycle is called the lunar node cycle.

The Solar Return chart is created when the Sun returns to the degree and minute it was in the natal chart. The Solar Return chart has special significance for grownups because it represents your intentions for the year based on the current energy.

Surges of energy, events, or actions linked to natal planets occur at return times. A return time is associated with a time when the planet speeds forward in the solar system. Important events can occur during these windows of activity and change. To interpret a Solar Return chart, combine your natal chart with celestial data. This includes the current house position of the planet, the zodiac sign, and its aspects to other planets in your natal chart.

While looking at these patterns on the Solar Return chart, look for creative and productive avenues to use your talents and energy. When you have a current transit linked to two planets and for which your natal chart relates these planets, you have a great chance at success. To achieve success, you can start or reassess projects professionally or artistically.

Even transiting planets influence the natal chart. For example, a transiting Neptune may attract you to someone who radiates the spirit and qualities of Neptune in your natal chart. Often the transiting planets can energize our lives and make old ideas seem new, inspiring us for old projects that have lost their spark and energy.

The time planets are near the sun is called planetary hour. Astrologically, planetary hours change every month, and because they are linked to the planet to which they refer, they can indicate events. An astrological birth chart's houses describe your nature and position in the family.

Chapter 10: Your Zodiac Sign's Qualities

A birth chart can indicate the work most fulfilling and complement a person's unique talents and abilities. An astrological consultation can ensure you're using your power to improve the world.

Consider the sign and house placement of the sign's ruler on the midheaven or cusp of the tenth house in your natal chart to get a clear picture of your career path. Your natal chart's ruler is the zodiac sign on the cusp of the ascendant, the zodiacal degree symbolizing your place of birth.

Aries

Aries thrive in fast-paced, competitive environments and are fearless straight shooters. They play to win and aren't afraid of taking the lead in business or relationships. Their aggressive energy and enthusiasm make them natural leaders. If you're an Aries, you likely gravitate towards leadership roles in the workplace. There's a chance that you're entering your peak career period now.

Aries at Work

The Aries boss is motivating, energetic, and a natural leader. They appreciate admiration and respect but can spot phony flattery in an instant. They're always go-getters willing to do what's necessary to get the job done.

People will gravitate towards their optimistic, honest, and energetic energy. Women with this zodiac sign are dedicated and aim to excel in their areas of expertise. They work hard, get things done, and prove their competence with accurate facts and figures.

If you give Aries employees autonomy and allow them to set their schedule and work style, they can be the hardest working and most dynamic employees. The Aries coworker is competitive and likes to be first, but they can be very inspiring when allowed to lead.

Aries' Inadequacies

Aries can be too bossy, quick-tempered, and competitive. People with these zodiacal traits are not open to criticism or perceived error. An Aries boss is often "in-over-their-heads," which can frustrate those around them. These overconfident individuals are often their own worst enemies when it comes to dealing with stressful situations. Although they can be powerful leaders, Aries bosses can sometimes clash with others and be overly results-oriented. So, it's not unusual to see a boss from Aries fire an employee, even unfairly. Thankfully, Aries doesn't hold grudges, and they appreciate people who share their drive to get ahead and cultivate success.

Taurus

Taurus bosses are builders who will tirelessly expand and grow whatever business or field they work in. They are calm and patient, but they can also be raging bulls. Taurus is a stubborn zodiac sign that resists change, preventing these driven individuals from keeping up with the latest trends in their fields.

Taurus at Work

The Taurus boss is patient, meticulous, and playful. They tend to take the long view and resist change because they don't believe it's necessary. Taurus bosses are sometimes seen as "the least innovative and most conservative people in the room, " which can be frustrating. Taurean bosses are creatures of habit who bring a sense of solidity and stability to their work and interpersonal relationships.

Taurus employees and coworkers are practical and realistic. They're very direct and aren't afraid to express themselves when they feel they aren't being treated fairly. As coworkers, they are pleasant to be around and assist self-starters with project completion.

Taurus' Inadequacies

Taurus bosses can be inward-looking, slow-moving, and resistant to change. These individuals focus on satisfying their goals at work and are uninterested in spending time networking or exploring new opportunities. Taurean bosses often find it difficult to motivate their team and delegate tasks effectively. So, when motivated, Taureans can be effective leaders creatively and effectively solve complex problems. So, their stubbornness and resistance to change can be their downfall.

Gemini

Geminis are chatty, interested, and mercurial and thrive in fast-paced environments. They are innovators and brilliant minds who publish often and read widely. They can create just about anything and aren't afraid to share their ideas with others.

Gemini at Work

A Gemini boss is unpredictable, restless, and always on the move. They are likable but will not get involved in workplace emotional dramas. Gemini is a flying sign—these folks are always running from one office to another and web-surfing or doing a tiny bit of everything at once.

A Gemini employee dislikes being confined and will become agitated if they are. They are good at absorbing information and can easily negotiate raises. Gemini employees, however, are not afraid to speak their minds even when it's contrary to the team's or individual's wishes. This can rile up both superiors and co-workers. They can sometimes become impulsive and unable to manage their tempers, which can frustrate any boss, but it's similar in most zodiac signs.

Gemini's Inadequacies

Gemini bosses can be too wishy-washy and lack the decisiveness to manage a business effectively. These bosses are typically disorganized and spend too much time thinking rather than taking action. Gemini workers hate monotony and routine and are easily bored or distracted.

Gemini is ruled by the planet of learning and communication, Mercury. These individuals are adaptable, think fast on their feet, and are curious about a fault. Geminis are curious and love to learn new things about the world.

Cancer

Cancer people are adaptable and nurturing and are best suited to careers caring for people or homes. These individuals can take on many roles at once and can handle pressure. Cancer people can be bossy and protective of those they love.

Cancerians at Work

Cancer bosses are strict about work ethics and reward their employees for their efforts. They're hardworking and will often take on projects without complaint. These folks excel at detail and could use more freedom in their roles.

If a Cancer employee has any emotional issues in their life, it will be difficult for them to keep them separate from their work. They are hardworking and dedicated and prefer jobs requiring emotional stability. These individuals are happy to work in emotionally-intensive fields. For example, they appreciate working with animals or patients.

Cancer's Inadequacies

Cancer bosses can be too kind or emotionally intense. They appreciate regular and open communication as much as avoiding conflict. If a Cancer boss becomes overly emotional while dealing with employees, they risk unnecessarily alienating their employees or staff. Cancer employees tend to get emotionally involved in their work and are often perfectionists. If a Cancer-sign employee becomes so absorbed in their work that it becomes overwhelming, they are likely to become depressed or stressed out.

Leo

Leos enjoy being the center of attention and are passionate, playful, creative, and entertaining. They thrive in careers that allow them to shine. They are boisterous but are easily distracted and sometimes pick unnecessary fights.

Leos at Work

Leo bosses are natural leaders who know how to delegate tasks to their teams. They need a lot of ego strokes and compliments and respond well to titles and status. Leos are competitive and ambitious. These folks are outspoken and often steal the spotlight. A Leo boss can be confident but knows how to promote their team's accomplishments. Leos's workplace environments are often creative and fun. A Leo boss will rally the team for a big project and rally the team for a celebration as well. These bosses are exceptionally good at motivating and retaining talent. Leo is generous with praise, and a Leo boss will relish telling others what they appreciate about their team's work.

When Leo employee works, they are eager to shine. They are ambitious and will do whatever it takes to reach their goals. Leos are good at delegating tasks and are often initiators, making plans for others to follow. As long as Leos understand how to avoid distractions and keep work projects organized, they will likely succeed in the workplace. Because of this, some Leo employers hire assistants to help them with organization, letting them focus on their jobs.

Leo's Inadequacies

When Leo feels threatened by his boss, they will sabotage or undermine him to get ahead. This is quite common in the workplace and will likely affect many of your colleagues. Leo bosses know how to spread work fairly among their team so that everyone gets a chance to prove themselves. But when it comes to their work, Leos can become ambitious and self-centered.

Virgo

Virgos are analytical and reflective, good at working with their hands, and good at planning, organizing, and getting things done. They are thorough and good at research and stretch out all projects well.

Virgos at Work

Virgos prefer careers that require them to use their critical and analytical skills, and they like to feel useful and meaningful. Virgos are detail-oriented and tend to micromanage, but they are not authoritarian and excel at crisis management. They are fair and expect to be fairly compensated, and they will hold you accountable for every detail of an employment contract.

Virgo coworkers are detail-oriented and will assist coworkers, but this can sometimes come across as critical and nitpicking. Virgos dislike conflict, and they avoid being associated with counterproductive behavior. If Virgos harmonize well in the workplace, they are reliable and organized coworkers who work well with others as long as the criticism is specific rather than personal. Virgos excel at research work and appreciate opportunities for learning on the job.

Virgo's Inadequacies

Virgos can be overly critical and nitpicky and focus on tiny details; this makes them vulnerable to big mistakes. Virgo coworkers can be extremely impatient, which can be difficult for some bosses to handle. This trait can be a problem when Virgo bosses don't socialize with their team enough to understand the needs and concerns of the employees under their watch.

Libra

Libras are deeply humanitarian and promote peace and harmony with others. They are diplomatic and fair-minded and usually keep their emotions in check to get ahead in the business world.

Librans at Work

The Libra employee brings a calming presence and diplomacy to any work situation and desires intellectual challenges. These employees tend to keep their emotions quiet at work and prefer to detach from their work. These individuals like to be social and have many friends, but only a select few they care about.

Libra bosses are focused on the best outcomes, even when they can be controversial. Libra bosses are skilled at helping the team brainstorm problems and find solutions. These individuals enjoy not being in the spotlight and like others to get some attention. These bosses are natural actors and enjoy role-playing and acting.

Librans' Inadequacies

People under the sign of Libra are friendly but lack consistency. They are gifted with communication but can be very selective about what information they want to release. Libra bosses expect a lot from their team and excellence, but they may not always be as devoted to their work as others. When making decisions, these bosses will weigh the interests of a party. They seem fair, but their focus is sometimes more on order and organization than serving the company's interests. Because of this, Libra bosses need excellent advisors who can provide sound guidance. Libra is a sign ruled by Venus, the ruler of love, beauty, and harmony.

Scorpio

Scorpios are passionate, driven, and intense. These individuals excel at objectives that involve intelligence, efficiency, or endurance. They prefer not to be emotionally invested in their work environment and don't like it when they have to pretend to be a certain type of person at work to advance at work.

Scorpios at Work

Scorpio bosses are strong-willed individuals who have mastered self-control. They are decisive and like to lead from the front, encouraging others to follow. They abhor laziness and inefficiency and tend to punish inefficiency with raises, promotions, or terminations. The Scorpio boss is intense and intimidating, but he will reward those deserving and talented. Their lack of trust can cause problems delegating tasks, lowering team productivity.

The Scorpio coworker has a strong presence and insight into the minds of their coworkers, but they don't reveal much about themselves. They understand the need to work and get things done. They are not afraid to stand up in the face of adversity and work hard to accomplish a task.

Scorpios' Inadequacies

Scorpios are single-minded, intense, and sensitive. They focus on the present rather than the future and lack empathy and compassion. These individuals like to avoid conflict and avoid making their coworkers feel pressured. They are also intense and focused on achievement, which can cause them to miss important details in their work. Scorpios don't share personal information with the other workers and don't trust others with their personal information.

Sagittarius

Sagittarius individuals, often filled with wanderlust, prefer a nomadic lifestyle and will be most fulfilled at work when traveling and moving. They may have difficulty being in one place for a long time.

Sagittarius at Work

The Sagittarius boss is enjoyable to work for and enjoyable to be around. They are forthright and honest, which may offend those around them, but their brilliant mind and keen approach triumph. Sagittarius bosses are effective but are indecisive, which can cause projects to take longer than necessary. These individuals have a strange level of loyalty to their coworkers that is rarely seen in bosses. They are devoted to their coworkers and give everyone a chance to prove themselves. They are natural leaders and promote teamwork among their coworkers.

Sagittarius coworkers are adaptable and are up for a challenge. They love to travel and seek adventure in their work life. A Sagittarius employee is reliable and trustworthy as a team member but may not be very organized. They are also ambitious and want to be respected for their industry expertise. People under the sign of Sagittarius are idealistic and believe they can achieve anything with effort and education. These individuals resist conflict and are not very good at expressing their emotions. They may need to learn some communication skills to motivate their coworkers in the workplace. Sagittarius bosses need to remember honesty in the workplace is not always the best policy.

Sagittarius' Inadequacies

Sagittarius isn't the most trustworthy sign. These individuals tend to overpromise and try to please their superiors, which may take away the entire team's productivity. Sagittarius' Inadequacies Sagittarius individuals are hard-working but do not always follow through, which can lower their credibility. These individuals tend to overestimate their capabilities and take the blame for things that aren't their fault. Not fully realizing their potential, Sagittarians may be only mediocre leaders. They prefer to let others take charge, insulating them from projects and leaving their team with less experience.

Capricorn

Capricorns are natural builders who enjoy constructing something solid and long-lasting, whether a structure, a career, or a business. These folks are natural team builders and know how to motivate team members to reach higher and achieve more.

Capricorns at Work

Capricorn bosses are dedicated, hardworking, and focused on their careers or business. They work long hours and effectively manage difficult clients and crisis situations. These individuals are highly diligent and are good strategists and planners. They also like to know exactly what they are doing and like stable and predictable things.

A Capricorn coworker is good at taking a difficult situation and remaining calm and collected. They are resourceful and independent, but they don't like to be micro-managed. They have a Medieval approach to leadership: "I lead you, you follow."

Capricorns' Inadequacies

Capricorns hate surprises, and even minor ones can disorient them. They can have trouble delegating tasks, choosing instead to do them themselves. They keep their emotions in check and rarely reveal themselves to others. People under the sign of Capricorn can be very family-oriented. Capricorns are very reserved and prefer things to be set as they are, though they can sometimes be flexible. They are sometimes not as good at communicating with their coworkers, which can cause their lack of participation in the workplace. They need to have open communication with their coworkers to expedite teamwork. Capricorn tries to control everything around them, even at work, which can lead to conflict or resentment with their team.

Aquarius

Aquarians are nonconformists and humanitarians, so they are best suited to academic careers. They are innovative but unpredictable and often create innovative work systems rather than following organizational practices.

Aquarius at Work

The Aquarius boss is a reformer and innovator who values intellect but is emotionally distant. They frequently work alone and are prone to forgetting minor details. They are also easy-going and driven by their passions and interests rather than their organizational responsibilities. These individuals are often innovative but also a daydreamer and can come off as selfish since they love to bask in their glory.

The Aquarius coworker is always interested in intellectual discussions and may attempt to persuade you to support their latest humanitarian cause. They have an independent spirit and prefer to work alone. They are unusual, bright individuals, and many love their coworkers for their uniqueness. Aquarius teammates get the job done but also like to have fun with their coworkers. Their innovative ideas often lead to creative workarounds that delight the Aquarius' boss.

Aquarius' Inadequacies

Aquarians are natural-born visionaries, but sometimes this can lead to unrealistic expectations of others. They have difficulty judging others' capabilities and often place too much value on their work. They are not good at delegating tasks since they are uncomfortable touching others' work. Instead, they prefer to handle each problem alone, sometimes leading to complications. They are impulsive and sometimes don't know how to express their emotions.

Pisces

People under the Pisces sign are imaginative and compassionate individuals who love working with people to help people. They are creative and enjoy problem-solving but don't like to maintain strict order or strict schedules.

Pisces at Work

The Pisces boss is a natural psychologist and works well in mental health and counseling. They can motivate individuals and give them the confidence they need to live a more fulfilled life. These individuals strive to make things pleasant and peaceful in the workplace. They are behind the scenes in leadership but know how to motivate their coworkers with kind words. They have a keen intuition, which helps them guide their team.

Pisces coworkers are creative and like to help others. They find joy in bringing people together to solve their problems. They enjoy hosting get-togethers and are good at communicating complex ideas to a wide audience. People under this sign must pursue a career that matches their sensitive nature.

Pisces' Inadequacies

Pisces bosses can be disorganized and forgetful at times. They are also hypersensitive and easily affected by their circumstances, so they take their work home. They also need to learn how to delegate tasks. Otherwise, they will burn themselves out or fail appropriately to meet their team's needs. Pisceans dislike noisy, challenging, and fast-paced environments.

Compatibility in Love

This section will give you a general overview of romantic compatibility for each zodiac sign. Just as each zodiac's business partners are different, so are each zodiac's romantic partners. Hence, your compatible horoscope may be a member of another zodiac sign with whom you have a strong sense of attraction and vice versa.

The Affectionate Aries

Aries are bold, direct, and forthright in love, and they will pursue their love with zeal. When they fall in love, they'll feel all-consuming. Their assertive demeanor can work for or against them in a relationship.

The sign Aries is ruled by Mars, the planet of war, and wants to assert dominance in the relationship. They're attracted to action movie heroes with the same confidence and strength.

- Aries women appreciate men who make their heart race. They are fiercely loyal in a relationship and wait until their man signals expressing his love to them; every emotional gesture is meaningful and exciting.
- Aries men are energetic and passionate but aren't afraid to be a bit overpowering. They're attracted to big-hearted women who cater to their every whim. For Aries men, looking good translates to feeling good, starting in the bedroom.

The Loving Taurus

A Taurus in love is devoted and persevering to the point of exhaustion to their partner. They commit to a long-term relationship and enjoy knowing their partner inside and out. To a Taurus, the intimate relationship is an active partnership that grows the more time and attention they devote to it. When Taurus falls in love, their egos are eclipsed by their devotion to their partner. People under this sign want a partner who will challenge and connect to them in meaningful ways.

Taurus is governed by Venus, the planet of beauty, wealth, and sexuality. Sensitive to beauty, money, and aesthetics, Taurus people are attracted to aesthetics in everything. They're drawn to a partner who appreciates their intelligence and practicality.

- Taurus women are drawn to physically attractive men who will be able to provide for them and be there for them in the future. A Taurus woman would opt for a sleek and sophisticated partner in relationships.
- Taurus men are intellectually and physically attracted to their partner and admire and appreciate her beauty. They're loyal and want to ensure their partner is well taken care of, emotionally and economically.

The Romantic Gemini

Geminis are quick, flirtatious, and pleasant; they consider their partner their best friend. They are fickle, exploring their options when their partner is unavailable. They only commit if they're sure the relationship is built to last.

Gemini is ruled by Mercury, the planet of communication and travel. Mercury likes change and likes to be around people because that's where it thrives. Gemini people are good at communication and finding common ground. Gemini people want to be around other people, but can become easily bored when paired with someone who isn't flexible or spontaneous.

- The Gemini woman is friendly and charismatic but often has various interests outside their romantic partner, and they may be ambivalent about romance. Because Mercury rules Gemini, they are attracted to intellectual partners who can keep up with their witty, inquisitive nature. Gemini ladies prefer light colors for their clothing and home décor to avoid dissipating their nervous energy.
- Gemini men are as equally driven and friendly as their Gemini counterparts. They enjoy having sex with their partner and provide this same flexible, spontaneous nature their lady loves. Gemini gents like staying active and fit.

The Affectionate Cancer

People under the Cancer sign are compassionate and will go to great lengths for their loved ones, but their loved ones must love them in return. These individuals want a partner who will look out for their interests and feel safe and protected with that person. To them, love is a commitment to shelter and emotional protection, which is why Cancer signs are most compatible with other Water signs.

Cancer is ruled by the Moon, which symbolizes emotional connections to the past and the future. Cancers have an innate sense of nostalgia and are drawn to a partner who sees beauty in the world. Cancer women are attracted to sensitive men who know how important it is to allow their girlfriend to have their own space. Cancer men are compassionate and know how to care for their loved ones and protect them. They want to provide for their lover financially and be there for her and the children.

- The Cancer woman is romantic and sentimental. She values stability and security in a long-term relationship and will wait for her partner to express his affection until she feels he's truly committed. She appreciates a man who sees the world through her eyes and greatly emphasizes communication, security, and stability.
- Men under the sign of Cancer are emotionally supportive and gentle but want to bond physically with their lover. They value their partner's emotional well-being and want to be by their side during good and bad times. Cancer males value loyalty and commitment in their relationships. To them, being in love is about being a couple and a family.

The Adoring Leo

People under the Leo sign are dramatic, energetic, and direct and will openly profess their love to a partner. Leos love to be adored and enjoy being in the spotlight. Leos deeply appreciates their significant other and expresses it in many ways. Leos also make love passionately and long for physical intimacy.

Leo is a sign ruled by the Sun, symbolizing strength and confidence. Leos are regal kings and queens of the zodiac and often take adversaries down with their metaphorical arrows. Leo reflects the Sun's power, often reflected in their clothing style and accomplishments. Leo represents ambition, pride, and success. Leos want to shine brightly in love and want a partner who will adore them as much as they would.

- The Leo woman adores her partner and openly expresses her love and affection. She's confident and needs her man to be just as confident as she is. Leo is a female sign ruled by the heart, so she's deeply romantic and kind and wants a man who can provide for her financially. She wants a man who appreciates her beauty and appreciates her accomplishments. These women will make beautiful mothers and wives.
- For Leo men, romance is about getting admiration and appreciation. They treat their partners like royalty and want them to be pampered. These men are confident and dignified and expect their partners to be the same.

The Devoted Virgo

Virgos are hard-working, idealistic intellectuals who are humanitarian by nature. A Virgo woman puts her lover on a pedestal and idealizes them. Virgos want a partner to provide with her and protect her financially. She's attracted to men with steady, structured jobs and respects her intelligence and good intentions.

Virgos are ruled by the planet Mercury, the planet of travel and communication. They value communication and are intellectually curious. Virgo people are friendly and pursue their interests as well as the interests of their significant other.

- A Virgo woman is deeply affectionate and loyal and wants a partner who shares the same qualities as her. She appreciates her partner's intellect and intellect and his involvement and commitment to the relationship and home life. She wants a dedicated partner who values her as a person, not just her physical beauty.

- Virgo men are introverted and analytical, preferring to analyze their partners rather than be emotionally direct with them. These men are highly committed and want to support their partners in all their endeavors, from emotional to professional.

The Caring Libra

Libras are diplomatic and interested in balancing partnerships to achieve harmony between them. These individuals are attracted to a partner who is as charming as they are and will balance their ego if their lover is too confident or agreeable. Libras like to relate to others and make their partner feel comfortable, which is why they're most compatible with Air signs.

Libra is an Air sign guided by Venus, the planet of love. Libras love and often pursue partners whose personalities are as confident as they are. Libras enjoy being in a relationship and being romantically involved. They have a great sense of humor and enjoy amusing and engaging in wittiness with their partners. Libras want to make their partners laugh and often put other suitors in their place, almost like a balancing act.

- Libra women are highly seductive, charming, and sensitive women who value balance and harmony in long-term relationships. They also appreciate the humor in their partners and put these men in their place when they feel too confident for their own good.

- Libra males are highly involved fathers and husbands who want to feel as connected to their partners and children as possible. Men under the Libra sign are also charming and witty and like making their partner laugh. They like romance and want to make their lady feel the same. These men quickly embrace a partner who makes them laugh and enjoys their wit.

The Fond Scorpio

People under the Scorpio sign are deeply emotional and devoted. To Scorpios, passion is one of the most powerful experiences you can have in life, which is why they're often drawn to partners who are just as passionate.

Scorpio is a deep and powerful Water sign governed by the planet Pluto, who symbolizes power and transformation. These individuals are passionate lovers who search for good companionship and company in their relationships. Scorpios find passion and power in long-term relationships and want to make their partners feel special and desirable.

- Scorpio women are loyal, passionate mothers who want nothing more than to make their families whole and happy. Females under this sign are sensitive and capable of accepting the truth, which is why they can spot lies and deceit in a relationship.
- Scorpio men are strong and protective of their lovers and will do anything to make a relationship work for the sake of the woman he loves. They want to make their homes comfortable but sensual, but they're also highly perceptive of the needs and emotions of their lovers and hold them to high standards. Scorpios want to feel loved and appreciated at all times and often seek a relationship where someone will be by their side.

The Supportive Sagittarius

Sagittarius is a high-energy, adventurous sign drawn to those with ambition and drive. These individuals appreciate a partner who is compassionate and connected to their many different interests.

Sagittarius people are ruled by the planet Jupiter, representing an expansion of one's interests and knowledge. Sagittarius is the sign of philosophy, philosophy class, and long-term philosophical conversations. Sagittarius is fun-loving but intellectual and likes to joke around with their partner or find entertainment together. They want to maintain a healthy relationship based on open communication and trust.

- Sagittarius women enjoy traveling and adventure and are charismatic and adventurous by nature. They pursue exciting but safe relationships with partners who understand their philosophy of life. Sagittarius women often seek equally intelligent partners and would rather sleep with someone intellectually stimulating. They're strong-willed and courageous in pursuing their relationships but need a strong partner who will support them emotionally and mentally.

- Men under this sign are also highly ambitious and value their independence.

The Warmhearted Capricorn

The Capricorn sign represents determination and control. These individuals appreciate the loyalty of partners who share the same goals and ambitions and are hardworking, disciplined, and persistent.

Capricorns are a highly ambitious sign ruled by the planet Saturn. People born under this sign are like the planet Saturn in many ways: they look forward to their conferences and plan and are highly organized. Capricorns appreciate taking their time to fall in love, but they are steadfast and devoted to their partner once they do.

- Capricorn women seek ambitious, responsible, and ambitious partners in their careers. These women are efficient, loyal, and reliable and want to find partners who are also practical and down-to-earth. They are cautious about their emotions and want a partner with the same traits and qualities.
- Capricorn men are very ambitious and want a partner with ambition and drive. These men love their independence and want their partners to respect this. Capricorns enjoy laughing together and finding common interests that make them a stronger team.

The Tender Aquarius

People under the Aquarius sign are creative and value equality. These individuals enjoy intellectual conversation and friendships. Aquarius people have a strong sense of right and wrong and can be emotionally distant.

Aquarius is an air sign ruled by the planet Uranus, representing originality and unpredictability. These individuals are philosophers at heart and are fascinated by philosophical questions. Like Uranus, Aquarians are unpredictable, contemplative and private people who value liberty and equality.

- Aquarian women are more ambitious and calculated when looking for love and prefer a long-term relationship that will eventually lead to marriage and family. These individuals want affectionate and passionate partners but can also be emotionally detached.

- Aquarian men seek partners who challenge them intellectually and make their partners feel valued. Men under this sign tend to be very open and communicative with their lovers and are more interested in subtle displays of affection and intimacy rather than overt displays of physical intimacy. Men under this sign focus on ideals rather than physical attraction and are more insightful than their counterparts.

-

The Big-Hearted Pisces

People under the deeply spiritual Pisces sign are some of the most romantic beings the world has ever seen. These individuals are highly intuitive and drawn to partners who have strong values and morals.

Pisces is a mysterious Water sign ruled by the planet Neptune, who represents self-deception and intuition. Pisceans are deeply romantic and want their partners to share their compassionate and warm personalities.

- Pisces women are often most interested in finding a supportive partner than someone physically attractive. These women are deeply compassionate and empathetic and want a partner to whom they can dedicate their lives. They don't often search for physical intimacy but instead seek a devoted partner who will share their interests and excitement about life.

- Pisces men are sensitive and emotionally connected to their partners. They're great comforters and ideal partners for people who desire a deep emotional connection and companionship.

•

Conclusion

Gendered astrological terms have traditionally been based on patriarchal myths and archetypes that conform to the binary, and Saturn has been portrayed as very masculine energy. However, in astrology, the planet Saturn represents feminity just as much as masculinity, and is inherently feminist and empowering.

Because patriarchal society values the masculine and devalues the feminine, the language used in traditional astrology interpretations has become binary and slanted. Perhaps it is time to reconsider changing the language so that the portrayal of feminine as good and light and masculine as evil and dark fades away.

Positive Affirmations – Part 1

Positive affirmations express the belief that a certain thing is possible. They can benefit anyone striving for a goal by teaching them to think positively. Some people read positive affirmations every day to achieve specific goals. You can benefit by repeating these simple statements to yourself to help you overcome negativity and succeed at your goals.

Repeating positive affirmations help you reach any goal you strive for by increasing your self-confidence, building a positive attitude, and boosting your determination. This helps you visualize your goal and realize the importance of reaching it. This can be any goal you have on your mind!

Affirmations can help you reach your goals faster. They involve repeating a phrase or statement until it becomes "second nature."

Now relax and calm down as you repeat each affirmation five times in a row for 2 minutes each. You will listen to the affirmation, and there will be a pause of 2 minutes after each affirmation to give you enough time to repeat the affirmation and let your brain process it.

I am grateful for the guidance that astrology provides.
Astrology is a powerful tool that I can use to improve my life.
I focus on the positive aspects of my astrological sign.
I am confident in my ability to interpret my astrological chart.
I use astrology to gain a deeper understanding of myself and my place in the world.
I am comfortable with myself and my astrological sign.
I am always connected to the universe and its energy.
My astrological sign helps me understand myself better.
I am grateful for the insight that astrology provides.

Astrology is a sacred experience, and I honor it as such.

I am open to all the possibilities that exist in astrology.

I have full faith in my ability to achieve anything I desire with astrology.

I am grateful for the insights that astrology brings me.

I am always amazed by the accuracy of astrology.

I can use astrology to create positive change in my life.

I am open to the possibility that everything is connected, including the stars and planets.

I am willing to accept that astrology may have something to offer me.

I am excited to explore the world of astrology.

I am curious about how astrology can help me in my life.

I am willing to learn about the different aspects of astrology.

I use astrology as a tool to gain insights into myself and others.

I trust in the guidance that astrology provides me.

Astrology is a useful tool that I can use to improve my life.

I am confident and secure in my astrological sign.

I know that my astrological sign is a powerful tool that I can use to improve my life.

I am excited to learn more about my astrological sign and to use its power to improve my life.

I focus on having positive, beneficial experiences with astrology.

I allow myself to be open and receptive to all the information I receive about astrology.

The universe supports me in all my endeavors.

I trust in the universe and its ability to guide me to my ultimate goals.

I am safe and secure in my astrological studies.

I release all worries and concerns to enjoy the experience of astrology to the fullest.

I am open to receiving all the guidance I desire about astrology.

In astrology, I have an unlimited ability to heal myself and others who need healing.

I am flexible and easily change my thinking to my choosing.

My mind is filled with positivity and dreams of success with astrology.

I can utilize the powers of astrology to manifest solutions to the problems in my waking life.

I have a limitless reservoir of energy, and this energy is put to good use when I study astrology.

I can manifest anything I can imagine in astrology with ease and grace.

I use my imagination to create anything I want in astrology.

I am in total control of my reality in astrology, and every experience and emotion is blissful.

The universe offers me opportunities to explore different aspects of astrology.

I gladly accept these opportunities to learn more about myself and the world around me.

My astrological studies take me to places I never thought of or imagined.

Every day, I find ways to improve my understanding of astrology so that I can get the most out of this experience in my life.

Every experience I have with astrology is another step in my journey toward creating the world I wish to live in.

With a positive and open mind, I am open and receptive to all the information I receive about astrology.

I cleanse myself daily, ridding my mind of negativity so I can be ready to receive all the positive information about astrology.

I create a sacred space for studying astrology and honor this space with deep reverence and love.

Every experience I have with astrology is rich with understanding and wisdom.

Every experience is viewed with love and compassion.

Astrology is my happy place. No matter what I learn, I always wake up with joy and excitement.

I honor myself in astrology with actions, thoughts, and feelings that make me feel great and good about myself.

My astrological studies are my most profound connection to who I am, and I am grateful to have this knowledge in my life. No matter how hard I try, I cannot change the nature of astrology

When I surrender to the infinite possibilities that exist in life, my astrological studies take me places I could never imagine going.

I have infinite opportunities when my mind is open.

I invite positive vibrations into my life and accept the information and guidance that comes my way.

I allow astrology to reveal itself to me.

My astrological studies are a reflection of my deepest desires, and I am determined to achieve them.

Positive Affirmations - Part 2

I am open to studying astrology every day, and I eagerly await each opportunity to learn more.

I have profound insights into astrology that help me understand my life better.

I use astrology to work through problems and figure out solutions.

I am fascinated by astrology and enjoy learning about myself through it.

My focus is on having positive, beneficial experiences with astrology.

I have complete faith in my ability to study and to understand astrology.

I am confident in my ability to read and interpret signs.

I have a natural talent for understanding the messages of the stars.

I am intuitive and can easily understand the language of the cosmos.

I am connected to the universe and can tap into its energy.

I am attuned to the vibrations of the Universe.

I am open to receiving guidance from the stars.

I trust in my ability to read and interpret signs.

I am gifted in the art of astrology.

I have a deep understanding of the energies at play in the cosmos.

I use astrology as a tool for self-discovery.

I use astrology to better understand myself and those around me.

I am always learning new things about astrology, and I enjoy expanding my knowledge.

Astrology is a valid tool for understanding yourself and your place in the world.

My practice of astrology is constantly evolving, and I am always learning new things about this ancient art.

I am excited to be on this journey of self-discovery through astrology.

I am keenly aware of the energies at play in my life.

I tune in to the cosmic flow and let it guide me.

I am attuned to the seasons and the rhythms of the cosmos.

I know that everything is connected, and I am a part of the web of life.

I listen to my intuition and trust my gut.

The stars align for me.

My actions are in alignment with my highest good.

My thoughts are positive and full of possibility.

I choose thoughts and actions that are in alignment with my highest good.

I know that I am the architect of my reality.

I am the captain of my ship, and I chart my own course.

I listen to my intuition and trust myself implicitly.

I follow my heart, and it leads me to amazing places.

The cosmos is conspiring in my favor.

Every day, I find ways to improve myself and my life.

All of the universe's energy is available to me to use as I wish.

The possibilities are endless for me.

I can achieve anything I set my mind to because I understand and utilize the power of manifestation correctly.

When I tap into the power of manifestation with focused attention, clear intent, and positive emotion, miracles happen in my life regularly.

I attract abundance and prosperity easily and effortlessly.

My cup overflows with all the good things life has to offer.

I live a charmed life because I choose to focus on what's working in my life.

Like attracts like, and I only attract positive things in my life.

I release all resistance to having what I desire, and it comes to me quickly and easily.

I allow myself to receive all the good things life has to offer me.

I am worthy of abundance in all areas of my life.

I open myself up to limitless possibilities by releasing all self-imposed limitations.

Astrology is an interesting way for me to get insights into my personality, relationships, and life path.

Astrology is one tool that I use to gain a greater understanding of myself and those around me.

I use astrology as a guidepost for making decisions in my life.

My astrological chart is a map of my soul's journey through this lifetime.

I interpret my astrological chart with accuracy and clarity.

I understand the messages that my astrological chart is trying to tell me.

My astrological sign describes some of my personality traits, but it does not define me.

I use astrology as a way to get in touch with my higher self.

I use astrology as a way to connect with the divine.

I am attuned to the energies of the universe.

I understand the ebbs and flows of life.

The cosmos is always conspiring in my favor.

Guided Meditation

Begin by lying down, letting yourself get comfortable, ideally flat on your back with your spine straight, legs uncrossed, arms at your side, palms facing open, however, if that is not comfortable for you, make comfort your priority and when you're ready, lovingly close your eyes.

Invite your awareness in words.

Tuning into your own inner landscape.

Feeling your breath.

Inviting it to flow as softly and naturally as it wishes.

Relaxing and allowing gravity to take over.

It's safe to let go.

To release into relaxation.

Now think about your intention for this practice.

Why do you want to explore your astrology?

What is it that you hope to achieve?

Allow yourself to really feel into your intention.

And as you do, begin to see yourself surrounded by stars.

You are completely surrounded by a blanket of stars.

And you may begin to feel as though you are floating amongst them.

You are safe.

You are held.

And you may begin to feel a sense of wonder and awe.

Allow yourself to really feel into the experience.

And as you do, you may find that you can begin to understand the language of the stars.

You may begin to see patterns and messages.

And you may begin to feel as though you are receiving guidance.

Trust what you are experiencing.

And begin to feel yourself merging with this imagery.

You see yourself as a part of the stars.

And you may begin to feel almost a sense of blissful ease.

And nothingness at all, Almost.

You are able to understand the messages of the stars.

And you may find that you can receive guidance and direction from them.

And when you are ready to come out of this practice, do so by first letting your awareness come back to where your body is right now.

Imagining roots anchoring you to the Earth, growing all along.

Either your back, in the back of your body, if you're lying down on your back, or whatever other part of your body is currently facing the Earth.

Just imagine, from your current angle, many roots are growing out of you.

And deep into the earth.

Allow yourself to imagine you are discharging any excess energy down, down through these roots, and letting that energy nurture the Earth as you only hold on to that which is for your highest, most loving good for now, to carry with you.

Moving forward and begin to really feel your body here now, noticing the points of contact between you and the surface on which you are resting.

And when you are ready, very slowly roll your shoulders, wiggle your fingers and your toes.

And only when you're ready.

Take your time as you open your eyes back to the world around you.

Thank you, namaste.

Freebies!

I have a **special treat for you**! You can access exclusive bonuses I created specifically for my readers at the following link! The link will redirect you to a webpage containing all my books and bonuses for each book. Just select the book you have purchased and check the bonuses!

>> https://smartpa.ge/MelissaGomes<<

OR scan the QR Code with your phone's camera

Bonus 1: Free Workbook - Value 12.95$

This **workbook** will guide you with **specific questions** and give you all the space you need to write down the answers. Taking time for **self-reflection** is extremely valuable, especially when looking to develop new skills and **learn** new concepts. I highly suggest you *grab this complimentary workbook for yourself*, as it will help you gain clarity on your goals. Some authors like to sell the workbook, but I think giving it away for free is the perfect way to say **"thank you" to my readers**.

Bonus 2: Free Book - Value 12.95$

Grab a **free short book** with **22+ Techniques for Meditation**. The book will introduce you to a range of meditation practices you can use to help you develop your inner awareness, inner calm, and overall sense of well-being. You will also learn how to begin a meditation practice that works for you regardless of your schedule. These meditation techniques work for everyone, regardless of age or fitness level. Check it out at the link below!

Bonus 3: Free audiobook - Value 14.95$

If you love listening to audiobooks on the go or would enjoy a narration as you read along, I have great news for you. You can download the audiobook version of *my books* for **FREE** just by signing up for a FREE trial! You can find the audio versions of my books (depending on availability) at the following link.

Join my Review Team!

Are you an avid reader looking to have more insights into spirituality? Do you want to get free books in exchange for an honest review? You can do so by joining my Review Team! You will get priority access to my books before they are released. You only need to follow me on Booksprout, and you will get notified every time a new Review Copy is available for my latest release!

For all the Freebies, visit the following link:

>> https://smartpa.ge/MelissaGomes<<

OR scan the QR Code with your phone's camera

I'm here because of you

When you're supporting an independent author,
you're supporting a dream. Please leave
an honest review by scanning
the QR code below and clicking on the "Leave a Review" Button.

★★★★★

https://smartpa.ge/MelissaGomes

Printed in Great Britain
by Amazon